Augustus George Legge

**Ancient Churchwardens' Accounts in the Parish of North Elmham**

From A.D. 1539 to A.D. 1577

Augustus George Legge

**Ancient Churchwardens' Accounts in the Parish of North Elmham**
*From A.D. 1539 to A.D. 1577*

ISBN/EAN: 9783337162344

Printed in Europe, USA, Canada, Australia, Japan

Cover: Foto ©ninafisch / pixelio.de

More available books at **www.hansebooks.com**

ANCIENT

# Churchwardens' Accounts

IN THE

## PARISH OF NORTH ELMHAM,

FROM A.D. 1539 TO A.D. 1577.

WITH DESCRIPTIVE NOTES AND A GLOSSARY

BY

AUGUSTUS GEORGE LEGGE, M.A.,

Vicar,

AUTHOR OF "THE ANCIENT ELMHAM REGISTER."

Norwich :
AGAS H. GOOSE, RAMPANT HORSE STREET.
1891.

# CONTENTS.

---

# INTRODUCTION.

HE following pages, a transcript of the earliest Churchwardens' Accounts in the possession of the Parish of North Elmham, derive no inconsiderable interest from the fact that they begin at the time (1539) when Thomas, Lord Crumwell, Henry VIII.'s Vicegerent, held sway in the Parish as Lord of the Manor of Nowers— in other words, he owned what is now known as the Elmham Estate. They show, amongst other matters of import, how rigidly the Reformation was here carried out. The ancient Church Plate is sold; the High Altar, Sepulchre, and Images of Saints are removed; the Books of the old Service are taken to Norwich; and a "Ministering Table," together with a form for the Communicants to sit upon, is set up in the midst of the Choir. In the reign of Mary, the books of the English Service are in turn ejected.

In the published Preface to the *Ancient Register*, I have already placed on record a brief sketch of parochial history, which it will be unnecessary to repeat here. But

as the following Accounts are mainly concerned with the
Church, it will be of interest to make some allusion to
the building itself.   Built, as it is, upon the highest ground
in the Parish, it becomes an attractive object to the eye
from a considerable distance, though the great length of
the Nave serves rather to dwarf the height of the Tower,
which presents in other respects a sightly and massive
appearance.   The style is good early Perpendicular, and
it is surmounted by a battlement and pinnacles, with an
extinguisher-like spire,—a modern addition which had been
better omitted.   Entering by the Tower, the visitor passes
through a Galilee Porch, enriched with roses, trefoils, &c.
Overhead are some mutilated figures, which, as the Church
is dedicated to S. Mary, may have been intended to represent
the Annunciation; on either side two huge gurgoyles mount
guard.   On the left, just within the doorway, will be seen
three early English stalls, having miserere seats.   At the
restoration of the Church in 1882, copies of these were
made and placed north and south on either side of the
Chancel.

A massive Elizabethan\* Screen separates the Tower from
the Nave, which is reached by (what, perhaps, is somewhat
uncommon) a descent of several steps.   From the top of

---

\* My authority for this is the late Mr. Phipson, who was employed as Architect in 1882,
but I am of opinion that the Screen is Jacobean, and not Elizabethan.   There are two
entries in the Churchwardens' Accounts which would seem to confirm this:—(1) in
1624, "I<sup>s</sup> p<sup>d</sup> to ffrancs floid for his work about the pticõn (partition) betweene the
steeple & the church, xxs."; and (2) in 1625, "I<sup>s</sup> p<sup>d</sup> to ffrancos fluid for workinge the
frame betweene the church & the steeple, xs."

these a full view of all the architectural beauties of the Church may be obtained. The Nave is 173 ft. in length, and, including the north and south Aisles, 43½ ft. in width. It is lofty, in six bays, the arches being supported by early English pillars, alternately round and octagon. Above is the Clerestory, having a triple-lighted window over each arch. There is also a window over the Chancel arch, looking east. Each Aisle is lighted by five double windows, with Decorated tracery in the heads. The western-most one on the south side differs from the rest, being three-lighted and Perpendicular. The Nave has fortunately retained the original ancient benches with richly-carved ends and poppy-heads. Towards the upper end new ones, after the model of the old, and prepared by the skilful hands of Messrs. Cornish and Gaymer of North Walsham, took the place of pews at the restoration of 1882. At the same time the pews in the Chancel were removed, and the stalls, to which I have before alluded, and Choir seats, the carving of which will delight the most critical eye, were introduced.

The attention of the lover of antiquity will be drawn to the beautiful Jacobean Pulpit standing on the south-west side of the Chancel arch. An interesting history is attached to it. It was made and carved by Francis Fluit, Fluide, or Floyde, who, as stated in a note in the Register Book, "began to be clark y° 24 of June, 1605." He was Clerk for forty-six years, and if famous as a skilled workman during his life, he was certainly as remarkable in his death. His burial took place on the 29th of August, 1651, and "he was foure score and tooe years of age *the day he was buried.*" In 1614 there is an entry in another Churchwardens' Book, "It⁹ pᵈ to ffrancs fluid for making yᵉ pulpit, xxs.," and again in 1626, "for finishinge the pulpitt, iiij*li.* iij*s.* iiij*d.*;" it would seem, therefore, that the labour of carving it took him twelve years to complete. In the vestry, forming the door to a cupboard, is an exquisite piece of his workmanship; it originally supported the sounding board, and has cut upon it the words, "Francis Floyde me fecit, A.D. 1626." On the Pulpit front will be noticed the very appropriate motto, *Verbum Dei manet in eternum.*

Some years ago, about 1851, when a former so-called restoration took place—Mr. Carthew, in the *Hundred of Launditch*, says he can scarcely speak of it with patience— this ancient work of art was cast out, pronounced by the then architect to be *rotten.* Mr. Barlow, the late Rector of West Toftrees, happily rescued it from destruction, and obtained permission to set it up in his own Church. At the restoration of 1882 he magnanimously returned it to the Parish, and, so far from being rotten, the workmen who did some slight necessary repairs to it found the wood hard enough to *break their tools.* But the Pulpit is not the only memorial of Francis Floyde's handiwork. The skilfulness of the same hand is to be traced on the Altar Table. The front is finely carved with grapes and vine leaves, and in the centre are the words, *Vera Vitis Chrsts*, with the date 1622, in which year occurs the following entry in the Churchwardens' Book:—"I? p^d to ffrancs fluid for making the comunion table for goold & cullers & other things as appeers by his bill, xxxiiij*s*."

In 1624 he made a journey to King's Lynn in order to see a free mason about a new Font, which cost the Church fund lx*s*. It was brought from Lynn in 1625, but does not appear to have been set up until the following year, when he is paid iij*s*. iiij*d*. for "leaddinge" it, and xiiij*d*. for "hewinge the (Purbeck) marble" which formed the base. It originally stood upon three steps, but unfortunately did not escape the spoiler's hand in 1851, when it was reduced to its present mean form. The Altar Rails were made and set up in 1685, and, like the Font, were considered to be too high, and were cut down at the same period of desecration. If the Pulpit had its vicissitudes, certainly, and even more so, had the Rood Screen. Sawn asunder in obedience to the injunctions of Elizabeth, and hacked about by the Puritanic frenzy of the Commonwealth, what little of it remained *in situ* was banished to out-of-the-way parts of the Church till 1851. Portions of it were then discovered, face downwards, flooring some of the pews. The relics have now been placed in their original position at the entrance to the Chancel, and enough is left to show how exquisitely beautiful it must have been in the days of its prime, when, no doubt, it extended from north to south of the Church.

The dimensions of the Chancel are about 42 ft. 3 in., by 18 ft. 7 in., and the thickness of the walls 2 ft. 8 in. High

up in the south wall, close under the roof, and looking into
the adjoining Chapel of S. James, is a small round-headed
Norman arch, broadly splayed inwards, and terminating in a
narrow aperture. Mr. Carthew mentions another of the same
size and character on the opposite wall, but in this he is in
error. There are traces, however, of another on the same
side, and near to the existing one. The Sedilia and double
Piscina are original, and are good bold specimens. The
priest's door is introduced in a very singular manner,
diagonally, across the angle formed by the south wall of the
Chancel and the east wall of the Chapel, at the west end of
which formerly stood the Rood Staircase, built out upon the
exterior wall. Alas! in 1851 the itching fingers of the
spoiler could not rest till it was taken clean away. Here, in
the Chancel, may be seen the oldest part of the Church. The
piers of the arches opening on either side into the north and
south Chapels (the former dedicated to S. John and the latter
to S. James) are of Norman style, and no doubt are the
remains of Bishop Herbert de Losinga's work, who is known
to have built a Church at Elmham. The Chancel is separated
from the Chapels by two light and beautifully-carved Screens,
placed there in 1882. At the west end of the Church two
boards record the names of the Bishops of Dunwich,
Elmham, Thetford, and Norwich. The roofs are plain open
Perpendicular.

Passing to the exterior of the Church, the south doorway
is Early English, with a plain Decorated porch. The north
doorway is the same date, early English, with a very singular

corbel table over it, supporting a horizontal projection. Mr. Carthew expresses himself to be puzzled by it. It appears to be composed of ornamental stones taken from another building, and I have no doubt myself that these fragments originally came from the ruins of Walsingham Abbey, whence, as will be seen in the following pages, stones were conveyed for the repairs of the Church.*

With reference to the restoration which took place in 1882, I shall be pardoned if, with some feelings of honest pride, I quote, word for word, from the lips of an unknown visitor to the Church in October, 1886, whose impressions of the manner in which it was carried out appeared in a local paper with the signature of "Linder" attached to it. He says :— "The next day, a very short journey (i.e., from Lowestoft) will take the rambler to North Elmham, and there he will find a Church which will well repay his visit, though the village is a very quiet one, and none would imagine, from a cursory glance, that it had contained a Castle as well as a Cathedral. The latter was a wooden one certainly, but still it was a Cathedral, and the place was a favourite residence of the Bishops; but the tide of life has surged over this place as completely as the sea over Dunwich, and but few take an interest in its existence. On entering the Church, the depth of it seems first to strike the eye. Several steps have to be descended, but when this is done, the only feeling is one of unfeigned admiration. Everything has been done that pride

* For this slight sketch of the Church's history I am mainly indebted to Mr. Carthew's *Hundred of Launditch*, from which I have made copious extracts.

and affection could do for a lovely Church. Almost the first
thing the visitor sees is a list of the Bishops of Dunwich and
Elmham. Bisus, the fourth Bishop, divided the See in 673,
making this the seat of the Bishops of Norfolk, while Dunwich
remained the seat of the Bishops of Suffolk. Those curious
names, what a history they are in themselves! Their very
dust, where is it? Some, doubtless, carried by the sea to
unknown regions : and still, they, being dead, yet speak.
The carving here is most beautiful. It has been copied, as
closely as possible, from the original; and well has the
design been carried out. The beautiful Screen has been
restored to its place ; but when we are told that it was
discovered under the floor of the pews, we marvel that it
was not lost altogether, as well as the priceless Pulpit
which was thrown amongst a heap of rubbish in a yard, and
only saved by an energetic Rector picking it out and carrying
it to his own Church, where it remained in safety till it was
claimed and welcomed back at the restoration. We will not
say the last restoration, for the one before was not worthy
the name. We could spend hours in this place, and we think
all true lovers of Churches will say the same after their
visit. Besides, there is a great deal that is interesting to the
archæologist in the Vicarage grounds. But we think enough
has been said to show that many happy hours might be spent
there.''

And now just one word, in conclusion, to those whose eyes,
whether archæological or otherwise, may happen to light
upon these pages. I absolutely refuse to lay any, the

smallest, claim to the exalted title of antiquary. I am only a mere tyro, a simple *amator temporis acti*, a lover of the past. The critic, especially if he be of bilious temperament, will no doubt discover many faults, although I trust a lack of seemly modesty on the part of the writer will not be one of them. If faults there be, as no doubt there are, I can only submit that, in conjunction with other erring mortals, I do but suffer from a disease which experience shows to be more chronic than epidemic, namely, ignorance. The notes which will be found at the end of the volume will give no new information to the advanced antiquarian; but as many have neither the taste nor the opportunity for the study of antiquities, and that amongst these some perhaps of my own parishioners may take an interest in these pages, I have proceeded, in the preparation of the work, on a principle for the application of which I have the high authority of Dr. Jessopp. In an article upon *The Manor of Aston*, which lately appeared from his pen in the *Nineteenth Century*, he makes the following, as I think, sensible remarks:—" A specialist is not always the best instructor even in his own subject; he is apt to forget that he was himself at one time a beginner, and apt to take it for granted that everybody knows this or that;" and he concludes in words which I would here take as my own, "In the following pages I assume no special knowledge on the part of whomsoever may attend to me."

Amongst many kind friends who have readily given me help in the preparation of this work for the press, and to whom my grateful thanks are due, I would especially mention the names of the Rev. William Hudson, one of the Secretaries to the Norfolk Archæological Society, and Mr. Robert Clarke, of the Norwich Diocesan Registry.

A. G. L.

# Bishops of North Elmham.

The following is taken from the learned work on *Episcopal Succession in England*, by Dr. Stubbs, Bishop of Oxford:—

The early East Anglian See was seated at Dunwich, in Suffolk. Felix, a Burgundian, having converted the kingdom, or, according to Camden, having brought it back again to the faith, became the first Bishop, A.D. 630. Fourth in succession to him, A.D. 669, was Bisus, or Bisi. He divided the See, placing one of the episcopal seats at North Elmham, in Norfolk. It has, indeed, been suggested that South Elmham, in Suffolk, was the place which he selected; but, besides the fact that all the best authorities are against this theory, there is this remark to be made, which would seem to go far to settle the question. Is it likely that Bisus would have placed two Sees in the same county, and so left the large and important county of Norfolk without episcopal supervision?

After the division of the See the succession of Bishops at Elmham was as follows:—

A.D.
673. Bedwin, or Bedwinus, the first Bishop.
693. Northbert, or Northbertus.
731. Headulac, or Huellæc.
736. Edilfrid, or Edilfridus.
758. Lanferth, or Lanferthus, or Eanfrith.

B

A.D.
781. Athelwulf, or Athelwolfus.
785. Humferth, or Alearus, or Alheard.
816. Sybba.
        Alherd, or Alherdus.
826. Humbyret, or Hunferth (martyred by the Danes).
845. Ethelwald.

During the Danish occupation of East Anglia all episcopal records perished, and no mention of Bishops, either of Dunwich or Elmham, occurs for upwards of a century. It seems, however, that in the tenth century the two Sees were re-united under the ancient title of the Bishopric of Elmham. We then find the following succession of Bishops:—

A.D.
942. Athulf, or Athulfus, or Eadulf.
964. Alfrid, or Alfridus, or Alfric.
964. Theodred, or Theodredus I.
980. Theodred, or Theodredus II.
995. Athelstan, or Ethelstanus, or Elfstan.
1001. Algare, or Algarus.
1020. Alwyn, or Alwynus.
1038. Alfric, Alfricus, or Elfric.
        Alyfrey, or Alifreius.
1043. Stigand, or Stigandus.
1047. Ethelmar, or Egelmarus.
1070. Herfast, last Bishop of Elmham, and first Bishop of Thetford, whither the See was transferred in 1075.
        The last Bishop of Thetford and first of Norwich (1091) was Herbert de Losinga.

# Vicars of North Elmham.

*Date of Institution.*

4 kal. Oct., 1305.   Walter de Blacolvesle vic. ad coll. Dni. Epi. pleno jure.

6 non Oct., 1311.   Richard de Aylsham, ad coll. Dni. Epi.

Prid. id. Apr., 1312.   John de Stanhow, ditto.

6 kal. Maij, 1328.   Richard de Kneshale, ditto.

5 Nov., 1344.   Edmund de Chevele (per mut. cum Betele), ditto. Joes de Cressingham.

8 Oct., 1354.   Roger de Felthorpe (Frettenham), ad coll. Dni. Epi.

17 Nov., 1355.   Olyv Wytton p mut. cum Worstede, ditto.

8 Jan., 1356.   Alan Attegar p mut. cum Heylesdon. Thomas Wentebrigg.

Pen. Dec., 1358.   Robert Percy, ad coll. Epi.

22 Aug., 1361.   George de Hoveden, ditto. Henry de Dunston.

21 Mart., 1367.   Richard de Blithe, ad coll. Dni. Epi.

11 Mart., 1410.   John Curtys de Diss, ditto.

15 Dec., 1412.   Walter Eston, ditto, officiale Jurisd. Maneriorum Dni. Epi.

1 Feb., 1427.   William Waller, ditto.

4 Mart., 1447.   John Bull, ad coll. William Malton, Vic.

26 Aug., 1449.   Simon Cosyn, ditto, eodem officiale.

20 Mart., 1489.   Hugo Kestren, ditto, Arch. Norv.

5 Oct., 1502.   Richard   Cooper,   ad   coll.   ejusd.   (Commissario
               Maneriorum).

22 Apr., 1523.  Richard Sylvestre, ditto.

16 Jan., 1541.  John Pecke, Epi. Capellanus, ad præs. Jac. Under-
               wood, raône prox. advoc.

4 Mart., 1559.  Joes Fysher, ad prœs. Ric. Fulmerston, arm. assign.
               Willi Epi. Norvic.
               Edmund Denny.

14 Oct., 1580.  Thomas Smith, ad prœs. Henrici Dni. Cromwell;
               1627, Archi. Norvic.

16 Sept., 1631. Nathaniel Ducket, ad præs. Edv. Coke, mil. (Cons.
               1636).

1 Nov., 1659.   William Wells, ad prœs. John Coke, mil. (Cons.
               1677).

5 Mart., 1680.  John Reed, ad præs. Rob. Harvey, arm.   Ob. Mart.,
               1703.

1 Mart., 1704.  Thomas Newson, ad prœs. Jois Harvey, arm.

Oct., 1719.    John Athill.

Apr., 1741.    Thomas Gregory.

Nov., 1777.    Thomas Herring.

July, 1828.    Charles Ford.

Jan., 1833.    Henry Edward Knatchbull (resigned 1867).

Apr., 1867.    Augustus George Legge, M.A., ad prœs. George
               John Milles, fourth Baron Sondes.

# Lands held by the Churchwardens.

---

Barker's Tenement lying at Catberd (see below).

Blackhurn Fyrlong, ½ Acre lying in.

Blomefeld's Close, j Acro lying at the west end of.

Brodslothe, ½ Acre lying at.

Camping Close, ij Acres called the.

Catberd Fyrlong, j½ Acre, copyhold, lying in.

Couerlecreste, j Acre lying in.

Edgegrave Fyrlong, j Acre lying in.

Fairstede, The.

Feld, xiij Acres of free land lying in diverse places in the.

Foster's Tenement, j Acre, copyhold, lying at Stretebusshes.

Foulde Course, The.

Fulfurth Dale (between Elmham and Gateley).

Heath, The Great.

Heath, The Little.

Heryng's Close, in Beetley.

Holgate, ij Acres, one free and one copyhold, lying at.

Johnson's Close at the Heath, j½ Acre lying in.

Parckegate, j Acre lying at.

Parckehyrne, j Acre and j Rood lying in.

Paynot's Deale, j½ Acre, copyhold, lying in and called.

Paynot's Tenement.

Pellet's Fyrlong, ½ Acre lying in.

Ramesley Townesend, j rood of free land lying at, and belonging to Norwich Priory.

Spylcok's Townesende, ij Acres lying at.

Stretebusshes, ½ Acre lying at.

Syluerdeane, j Acre lying at.

Taverner's Close, ½ Acre lying in.

Taverner's Great Close, j Acre, free, lying in.

Thornwell.

Town Carr, The, in Beetley and Gressenhall.

Town Close, The, in Beetley.

Well's Townesend, j Acre and j Rood lying at.

Wodcok's Close to yᵉ Bromward, ½ Acre lying in.

Woodforthe.

# Churchwarden's Accounts.

---

Receyts, Aº Dm̃, 1539.

| | | |
|---|---|---|
| **m.** | ffirst of yᵉ town att yᵉ acownts . . . . . | **xvj**s. j*d*. o**ƀ** |
| **9.** | Itm̃ reč of yᵉ v pownds yᵗ Richard Pers gafe to yᵉ⎫ chirch at dyu⁹se tymes . . . . .⎬ | **lv**s. |
| **31°** | | |
| **ſIII.**⎤ | It. reč of yᵉ Vicar yᵗ he had of corpis Xⁿ gyld ⁽¹⁾ . | **iiij**s. **iiij***d*. |
| | It. of Will yarã for lond ferme ⁽²⁾ of yᵉ last yer . | **ij**s. |
| | It. att yᵉ rekenyng att hallowmes ⁽³⁾ for yᵉ dr̃ykyng,⎫ ɀ of yᵉ stok, ɀ for lond ferme . . . .⎬ | **xv**s. **viij***d*. o**ƀ** |
| | It. of John Taûner ⁽⁴⁾ for j acr⁹ ɀ an halfe of lond ferme | **xij***d*. |
| | It. of dyu⁹se psons for c̃ten candilstykks sold to them . | **iij**s. **xj***d*. o**ƀ** |
| | It. of Will lusher for ij acres of lond yᵉ cãpyng⎫ close ⁽⁵⁾ . . . . . . . .⎬ | **xx***d*. |
| | It. of Nicħus Purdy for ij acr⁹ of lond . . | **xvj***d*. |
| | It. of yᵉ Vicar for ij bɜ ɀ an halfe of morter . . | **iij***d*. |
| | It. reč of Sʳ John Elverich ⁽⁶⁾ of mony yᵗ be left of⎫ mc̃dyng yᵉ clok . . . . . . .⎬ | **iij***d*. |
| | It. reč of Nicholas Dyth for an old cow yᵗ he had of⎫ John Penyall, wᶜʰ was sũtyme longyng to corpis⎬ Xⁿ Gylde . . . . . . .⎭ | **vij**ₛ. |

It. reč yᵉ rest of yᵉ mony yᵗ Rič Pers gafe to yᵉ chirch   xlvs.

It. of Petyr Carter . . . . . .        iiijd.

It. of Galfrey Rud for lond ferme . . . .     xd.

Sm̃ toˡˢ, vijli. xiiijs. ixd. ob

Payed.

In pᵒmis to yᵉ stolers for bred ȝ drynk whan they⎫
  gathered stones . . . . . . .⎭   ijd.

It. to Nicħus Purdy yᵗ he had forgotyn at yᵉ rekenyng⎫
  for sond carryyng . . . . . .⎭   vjd.

It. for iij hũdred yerne . . . . . . xviijs.

For caryyng home of yᵉ yern . . . . .    vd.

It. Nicħus Ɖyth for caryyng of iij lode of ston . .   xviijd.

It. for remouyng, leyyng, ȝ sowdyng of sent James⎫
  chappell . . . . . . . .⎭   vs.

for nayle . . . . . . . . .   iijd.

for wood . . . . . . . . .    id.

It. ij plomers oon day, mendyng of yᵉ chirch elys ȝ⎫
  sent Johns chappell . . . . . .⎭   viijd.

for ijli. of sowd . . . . . . . .   viijd.

for ther bord . . . . . . .    vd.

for wood . . . . . . . . .    jd.

It. for vj yards of Normãdy canvas for ij rochetts [7]   iijs.  vjd.

Itm̃ for a mason iij dayes mẽdyng of yᵉ chyrch walles .   xijd.

for hys ȝuyor yᵗ same tyme . . . .   vijd. ob

for ther expensys hetherward . . . .   ijd.

for ther bord yᵉ seyd iij dayes . . . .   xvd.

to will heer for a day ȝ a halfe to help thē . . .   iijd.

for hys bord . . . . . . . .   iijd. ob

for ij lode of sond caryyng . . . . .   vd.

Itm̃ to Edmund Stabylford for dyggyng ij pytts for⎫
  yᵉ g̃ts . . . . . . . . .⎭   xd.

It. to Reyner for cōveyyng a way of yᵉ menor⁽⁸⁾ for $\left.\right\}$ ij*d.*
yᵉ oũ grate . . . . . . .

Itm̃ to Jamys Rūmer yᵉ mason for makyng of ij grats $\left.\right\}$ ij*s.*
& mēdyng of chirche walles vj dayes . . .

to hys ꝰuyor vj dayes . . . . . . xv*d.*

for yᵖ bord for vj dayes . . . . . . ij*s.* vj*d.*

Itm̃ to Will yarā for yᵉ tȳbyr wark of both yᵉ grats . ix*s.*

It. for ij lokks for yᵉ chirch boxe . . ·. . iiij*d.*

Itm̃ payed for rent of lond longynge to yᵉ town . . vj*s.* vij*d.* oẞ

Itm̃ to Tylney for glasyng . . . . . xx*d.*

Itm̃ for a lode of flaggs g̃vyng & caryyng . . . iij*d.*

Itm̃ for removyng of yᵉ morter into yᵉ chirch . . j*d.*

It. to Robᵗ Ryall for yᵉ mēdynge of iij bell clapers . xiij*s.* vj*d.*

Itm payed to Will yarā for bordyng & latasyng of ij $\left.\right\}$ xij*s.*
of yᵉ stepyll wȳdows . . . . . .

Itm̃ yᵉ goodman pers had wherwᵗ he made yᵉ grate owt
of yᵉ chirch yard into yᵒ feyer stede⁽⁹⁾, both ston $\left.\right\}$ xxv*s.*
work, yerne & tȳbyr . . . . . .

Itm̃ to yᵉ bell hāger for hys ffee . . . . . viij*d.*

Itm̃ for lether for yᵉ bawdrykks . . . . . iiij*d.*

for hys wags yᵗ mad thē . . . . . iiij*d.*

for hys bord . . . . . . . ij*d.*

Itm̃ to heryng for rent yᵗ was nott payed whan he was $\left.\right\}$ x*d.*
coler . . . . . . . . .

Sm̃ to¹ˢ, v*li.* xij*s.* ix*d.* oẞ.

The sm̃ of yᵉ receyts . . . . . . vij*li.*xiiij*s.*ix*d.*oẞ

The sm̃ of yᵉ chargs . . . . . . v*li.* xij*s.* ix*d.* oẞ

& so yᵖ remayncth wᶜʰ ys her leyd down att yᵉ ac- $\left.\right\}$ xlij*s.*
cownts—mony . . . . . . .

& these chirchereves ar dischargyd for y¹ˢ yer.

c

10 CHURCHWARDENS' ACCOUNTS

M<sup>d</sup> aft ye rekenyng made, Will Rūmer hath chosen to be hys felow (1)
for thys yer comyng Richard Pers.

delyūyd to them in hand. . . . . . xlijs.

A° Dom.
1540.
[A° 32°
Hen.VIII.]

A° Dm̃ 1540.

The rent of ye town lond.*

In p⁹mis to ye howse of Carbrok for j acr⁹ of ffre lond ⎱ ijd.
lyyng in Taūners gret close . . . . ⎰

It. to M⁹ Mĩyn or to ye p̃or for j rod of fre lond lyyng ⎱ jd.
att Ramesley townesend . . . . . ⎰

It. to my lord (11) for j acr⁹ & di ten⁹ Paynott t⁹re ⎱ iiijd. oḃ
natie⁹ (12) lyyng att paynotts deele . . . ⎰

It. to my lord for j acr⁹ & di ten⁹ Barker t⁹re natie⁹ ⎱ iiijd. oḃ
lyyng at Oatberd . . . . . . ⎰

It. to my lord for j acr⁹ ten⁹ ffoster t⁹re natie⁹ lyyng ⎱ vd.
att strete busk . . . . . . . ⎰

It. to my lord for ij acr. callyd ye cāpyng close . . xxd.
It. to my lord for an halfe acr⁹ lyyng in Taūners close . ijd.
It. to my lord for xiij acr⁹ of ffre lond lyyng in diũse ⎱ 4s. 4d.
placs in ye feld . . . . . . . ⎰

⎧To ye howse of Carbrok (13) . . . ijd.
Sm̃ ⎨To M⁹ Mĩyn or to ye p⁹or (14) . . . jd.
⎩To my lord . . . . . . 7s. 4d.

rent. The town lond. ferme.

ijs. ijd. oḃ Thomas Shetyll hath vij acres and a rode ⎱ iiijs. xd.
payyng yerly . . . . . ⎰
viijd. Nicħus Purdy, ij acres . . . . xvjd.
xijd. Will lusher, iij acres . . . . . ijs. iiijd.
xd. oḃ Will Yarā, iij acres . . . . . ijs.

* This Rent Account is given at the end of the Book.

v*d.* Will ffrancklyng, j acr$^9$ 4*d.*, & a rode j*d.* . xij*d.*

iij*d.* John Taůner, j acr$^9$ j*d.*, & an halfe 2*d.* . xij*d.*

v*d.* Jaffrey Rudd, j acr$^9$ . . . . . x*d.*

xx*d.* Will lusher y$^e$ cāpyng close ij acres . . ij*s.*

The rent of town lands fre & copey is in all vij*s.* vij*d.*

s̃m t$^9$re { lib . . xiiij acr$^9$ & j rod
{ natie$^9$ . . vj acr$^9$ & dī

A° Dm̃, 1540.

M$^d$ a rekenyng made y$^e$ Wednesday in Whitson Weke y$^e$ yere of o$^r$ lord god M$^{ll}$ccccc xl$^{ti}$ of Richard Pers chirch Warden of Northelmhm̃ for hȳ & Will Rūmer [15] late deptyd (on whose sowle god hafe m̃cy).

Receyts.

In p$^9$m receyvyd of y$^e$ town at y$^e$ accownts . . . xlij*s.*

It. rec̃ of Edmund fflecher . . . . . . ij*s.*

It. for certon lawnds sold . . . . . . xv*d.*

It. rec̃ of y$^e$ drynkyn . . . . . . x*s.*

It. rec̃ y$^t$ same day of y$^e$ stokks of Gildes . . . iij*s.* vij*d.*

It. rec̃ att hallowmes drȳkyng . . . . . iiij*s.* iii*d.* oᵬ

It. rec̃ of m̃ fferro$^r$ [16] & Syr John Elverich pt of y$^e$) legacy of Henry Trc̄dell . . . . .} xx*s.*

It. receyvyd for ferme of y$^e$ town lond, y$^t$ ys to say, of Thom̃s Shetyll fõ vij acr$^9$ & a rode, iiij*s.* x*d.*; of Nich. Purdy for ij acr$^9$ xvj*d.*; of Will lusher for iij acr$^9$ ij*s.* It. of y$^e$ same Will lusher for y$^e$ cāpyng clos, ij*s.*;} xv*s.* of Will yarā for iij acr$^9$ ij*s.*; of Will ffranckelyng for j acr$^9$ & j rod, xij*d.*; of John Taůner for j acr$^9$ & dī, xij*d.*; of Jaffrey Rudd for j acr$^9$ x*d.* . .}

It. rec̃ of Edm̃nd fflecher . . . . . . x*s.*

S̃m to$^{ls}$, v*li.* viij*s.* ij*d.* oᵬ.

c 2

Payed.

M$^d$ that these be y$^e$ chargs & expēs$^9$ leyd owt & payed y$^e$ seid yer of o$^r$ lord god M$^{ll}$ccccc xl$^{ti}$ by y$^e$ seid Ric Pers and Will Rūmer, chirch Wardens.

In p$^9$mis payed to y$^e$ bekyn [17]   .    .    .    .    . ij$s$.

It. for Rent of j acr$^9$ of y$^e$ town lond to y$^e$ pctor of ⎫
sent John [18]   .    .    .    .    .    . ⎬   j$d$.

It. to M$^9$ fferro$^r$ for cowncell   .    .    .    . xx$d$.

It. for Washyng of y$^e$ chirch geer   .    .    . xvj$d$.

It. to Herry Wells for tēdyng of y$^e$ bells   .    . vj$d$.

It. payed to y$^e$ becon for y$^e$ Watch   .    .    . iiij$s$.

Redd$^t$ (i.e.     It. paye(d) to Edmnd Gogney, collector for rent for y$^e$ ⎫
Reditus,     town lond for thys yer .    .    .    . ⎬   vij$s$.

Rent).     It. y$^t$ Will Rūm had leyd owt   .    .    .    . xij$d$.

It. payed to Will Tylney for mēdyng of y$^e$ leed of y$^e$ ⎫
pynnacle   .    .    .    .    .    .. ⎬   xij$d$.

It. payed to Syr Joh Elverich for pchemyn for y$^e$ ⎫
Indentures of y$^e$ town lond .    .    .    . ⎬   iiij$d$.

It. payed to Will yarā for bordyng of y$^e$ stepyll ⎫
wyndow   .    .    .    .    .    .    . ⎬   iiij$d$.

Sm to$^{ls}$, xix$s$. iij$d$.


Itm to Wyllm lussher for mendyng & enlargyng of y$^e$ ⎫
Causye frō hys own howse to y$^e$ balyes [19]   . ⎬   vj$d$.

Itm to M$^9$ dethycke for y$^e$ rent of y$^e$ town londs   . vj$s$. j$d$. ob

Itm to Nycholas dyght for Caryeng of Grauell one ⎫
holl day w$^t$ hys own Carte for y$^e$ Causye by y$^e$ ⎬   xij$d$.
balyes   .    .    .    .    .    .    . ⎭

Itm to Thoms Shetell for Caryēg of Grauell y$^e$ same ⎫
day thyther   .    .    .    .    .    . ⎬   xij$d$.

Itm̃ to yarrhm̃ for bords for to make A shest to ley yn ⎫ ijs.  ijd.
the Comon lyght.[20] ɛ yᵉ makyng of yᵉ same . ⎭

Itm̃ for nayles for yᵉ seyd shest ɛ for yᵉ Chyrche gats . ijd. ob

Itm̃ to Wyltm Collys for yrons for yᵉ seyd shest . . ˙ xjd.

Itm̃ for ij locks, one for yᵉ seyd sheste, ɛ one for yᵉ ⎫ iiijd.
organs . . . . . . . . ⎭

Itm̃ to yᵉ fre masn of derhm̃ wyche hathe taken yᵉ ⎫
wyndowes in yᵉ Chyrche ɛ dyuse other thyngs ⎬ iiijd.
theronto belongyng to make . . . . ⎭

Itm̃ in Expenss for hym yᵉ same tyme at yᵉ balyes . jd.

Itm̃ delyūd to hym yᵉ same tyme afore hand vjs. viijd. ⎫ vjs. viijd.
to be Alowed ageyn whā he entre yᵉ seyd worcke . ⎭

Smm̃, xlvjs. iijd.


Aᵒ Dm̃ 1541ᵒ

Expenss leyd owte by Rychard pers aforseyd—

In p̃mis for A Syrples for yᵉ Vycar . . . . vjs. viijd.

Itm̃ for A Byble [21] for yᵉ towns pte . . . . iiijs.

Itm̃ for A lode of fre stone at Walsynghm̃ Abbey, [22] ⎫ xvjd.
wyche lye ther yet styll . . . . . ⎭

Itm̃ in Expenss at Walsynghm̃ whan they went to bye ⎫ vd.
yᵉ seyd fre stone ɛ other . . . . . ⎭

Itm̃ for yrons for yᵉ ij turnyng postes upon yᵉ Causye ⎫ vd.
by yᵉ balyes aforseyd . . . . . . ⎭

Itm̃ leyd owte to yᵉ taxe . . . . . . vs. iiijd.

Itm̃ to yᵉ masyng for goyng to Wāsynghm̃ wᵗ hym to ⎫ vjd.
see yᵉ fre stone aforseyd . . . . . ⎭

Itm̃ in Expenss whan we rod to Norwyche to see ye ⎫ ixd.
bells [23] at Mᵒ Ruggs for yᵉʳ horses ɛ them selues ⎭

Sum̃, xixs. vd.

the suṁe of yᵉ reč of Rychard heyward  .  vij*li.*  vijs. xi*d.* oᵬ
the Suṁe of yᵉ reč of Rychard pers  .  .  iij*li.*  vjs.  viij*d.*
the Suṁe of yᵉ Chargs of Ry. h.  .  .  . xlvjs.  iij*d.*
the Suṁe of yᵉ Chargs of Ry. pers  .  .  .  . xixs.  v*d.*
ȝ so remayn in yᵉ hands of Ry. heywarde as ys here ⎫
leyd down att yᵉ Acompts in monye  .  .  .⎬ v*li.* xxᵗˡ*d.* oᵬ
ȝ in yᵉ hands of Rychard pers remayn as ys leyd down ⎫
att yᵉ acompts in monye  .  .  .  .  .⎬ xlvijs.  iij*d.*
And in bothe ther hands ther remayn as ys aforseyd  vij*li.* viijs. xj*d.* oᵬ

et sic  And so these Chyrche wardens are dyscharged for thys
quieti sñt  yere.

Mᵈ. after yᵉ rekenyng made Rychard Heyward hathe chosen to be
hys felow for this yere comyng Thoṁs Powle.
Deliu⁹d them in hand  .  .  .  .  .  . vij*li.* viijs. xj*d.* oᵬ

A° Dm.  A° dṁ 1542°
1542.
[A° 34°  Mᵈ A Rekenyng the wedñseday yn whyghtsone weeke yᵉ yere of oʳ
Hen.VIII.]  lord god A ᴍ'ᶜᶜᶜᶜ xlijᵗˡ of Rychard Heyward the elder ȝ
Thoṁs Powle, Chyrchewardens of Northelmhṁ

The Receyts of me, Rychard Heyward, aforseyd.

In p⁹imis reč of the town at yᵉ Acompts  .  . vj*li.** viijs. xj*d.* oᵬ
Itṁ reč of Sʳ John Elūyche p⁹yst towarde the makyng ⎫
of yᵉ iiij Mydle panes of the grett wyndow yn ⎬ vjs.  viij*d.*
Seynt James Chapell wᵗ whygt glasse  .  .⎭
(Beetley  Itṁ reč of Robt. A. Sohṁe for yᵉ ferme of ij Acr⁹ of ⎫
ferme) B. f.  londs, ij yeres  .  .  .  .  .  .⎬ iiijs.

* Query vij*li.*, see above.

Itm̄ reč of Rychard Crow for yᵉ ferme of ij Acrᵍ of Medew, ij yers, vs. iiijd., whereof Alowed ageyn vnto hym for yᵉ rent of yᵉ seyd Medew ij yers, xijd.; ⅋ for fyeng of the dytches, xxd.; ⅋ so remayn yn myn hands all thyngs Alowed vnto hym, ijs. viijd. . . . . . . . . . . . . . . . . . . . . . . . . . . ijs. viijd.

ham  Itm̄ reč of Thom̄s lussher for yᵉ Campyng closse . ijs.

) E. f. Itm̄ reč of the same Thom̄s for iij Acrᵍ of londs yn yᵉ ffylde . . . . . . . . . . ijs.

E. f. Itm̄ reč of Herry Rustñ for londe ferme . . . ijs.

E. f. Itm̄ reč of Wyltm yarrhm̄ for lond ferme . . . ijs.

E. f. Itm̄ rcč for Halowmes nyght all thyngs dyscharged . vs. vjd.

E. f. Itm̄ reč of Nycholas purdy for lond ferme . . . xvjd.

B. f. Itm̄ reč of Mᵍ dythycke for lond ferme lyeng yn Betele vs. vjd.

E. f. Itm̄ reč of Thom̄s Shetell for vij Acrᵍ ⅋ j rode . . iiijs. xd.

E. f. Itm̄ reč of Wyllm̄ ffrankelyng for j Acrᵍ ⅋ one rode . xijd.

E. f. Itm̄ reč of Jaffry Rudd for j Acrᵍ of ferme lond . xd.

B. f.  Itm̄ rcč of Thom̄s Howsse of Bytteryng magna for pte of the ferme of A Certen closse wᵗin Betele . . vjs.

Itm̄ reč of Symond Newton of Norwyche, dwellyng yn Seynt Androwes pysshe for Certen plate (²⁴) aftᵍ iiijs. yᵉ vnce . . . . . . . . xxiijs.

Itm̄ reč of yᵉ same Symond for yᵉ Sylū yᵗ was vpon the Crosse yᵗ the relyques wheryn . . . . xixs. ijd.

Itm̄ reč of Mᵍ Nycholls for yᵉ sylū sheeos wyche wer vpon yᵉ brown rodes fete . . . . . xs.

Itm̄ reč of Edm̄nd ffletcher vjs. viijd., pcell of xiiijs. viijd. As yn yᵉ boke of yᵉ chyrche dett more playᵍly dothe apere . . . . . . vjs. viijd.

The wholl Sum̄e of yᵉ Receyts of me, Rychard Heyward aforseyd . . . . . ys xili. xiiijs. jd. oᵇ

These be the Expenss & Chargs leyd owte by me y<sup>e</sup> seyd Rycharde
Heywarde, one of y<sup>e</sup> Chyrchewardens of Nor(thelmham) y<sup>e</sup>
yere of o<sup>r</sup> lord aforeseyd.

| | | |
|---|---|---|
| In p<sup>9</sup>imis payed to M<sup>9</sup> Sydney, of Walsynghm̃ pua, for pyllors & other fre stone for y<sup>e</sup> wyndowes and butteres yn northellmhm̃  .    .    .    .    . | iijs. | vd. |
| Itm̃ to ij men for y<sup>e</sup> helpyng of yt down ther   .    . | | ijd. |
| Itm̃ to weston of walsynghm̃ for A Chalder of lyme | ijs. | xd. |
| Itm̃ yn Expenss ther the same tyme  .    .    .    . | | viijd. |
| Itm̃ for halfe A hũdered of iiijd. nayle   .    .    . | | ijd. |
| Itm̃ payed to Thom̃s Shetell for y<sup>e</sup> Caryeng of A Chalder of lyme .    .    .    .    .    .    . | | xxd. |
| Itm̃ to y<sup>e</sup> same Thom̃s for y<sup>e</sup> Caryeng of A lode of sonde  .    .    .    .    .    .    .    .    . | | iijd. |
| Itm̃ to John wodcoke for y<sup>e</sup> Caryeng of A Chalder of lyme  .    .    .    .    .    .    .    .    . | | xxd. |
| Itm̃ to Ry. Rustñ for the Caryeng of A lode of fre stone | | xxd. |
| Itm̃ to Rychard purdy for Mendyng of the barres of y<sup>e</sup> wyndow yn Seynt James Chapell   .    .    . | | xijd. |
| Itm̃ for ij<sup>li</sup> of pytche for to pytche y<sup>e</sup> barres of y<sup>e</sup> seyd wyndow  .    .    .    .    .    .    . | | ijd. |
| Itm̃ yn Expenss at Norwyche whan we went to setthe (?) bells  .    .    .    .    .    .    . | | xvjd. ob |
| Itm̃ to one to watche y<sup>e</sup> Chyrche whan y<sup>e</sup> wyndow of Seynt (James) Chapell was yn y<sup>e</sup> makyng and glasyng  .    .    .    .    .    .    . | | ijd. |
| Itm̃ to y<sup>e</sup> Masons Man at y<sup>e</sup> fyrst tyme for hys wags vij dayes  .    .    .    .    .    .    . | | xxjd. |
| Itm̃ to m̃ Rugge of Norwyche yn pte of paymẽt for y<sup>e</sup> bells   .      .    .    .    .    .    . | | vs. |

Itm̃ to Wyllm̃ Tylney for iiij panes of new glasse for
the wyndow yn Seynt Johns Chapell aft̃ iiijd. ob
yᵉ fote . . . . . . . .     xijs.   xjd.

Itm̃ to yᵉ same wyllm̃ for yᵉ takyng down of sex other
panes of yᵉ same wyndow, & for yᵉ storyng &
mendyng of them aft̃ vjd. A pane, iijs. ; but yᵉ    iijs.
led was owʳ own . . . . . . .

Sum̃, xxxvijs. xd. ob.

Itm̃ payed to yᵉ Mason at yᵉ fyrst tyme for iiij dayes
aft̃ vjd. yᵉ day . . . . . . : .    ijs.

Itm̃ to hys Man at yᵉ second tyme for ix dayes, aft̃
iijd. yᵉ daye . . . . . . .    ijs. iijd.

Itm̃ Alowyd to myselfe for ther Comons iij wekes, aft̃
xvd. yᶜ weke for yche of them . . . .    vijs. vjd.

Itm̃ to yᵉ Mason yᵉ second tyme for vj dayes, aft̃ vjd.
yᵉ day . . . . . . . . .    iijs.

Itm̃ to hys Man the seyd tyme, aft̃ iijd. the day . .    xviijd.

Itm̃ Alowed to myselfe for yᵉʳ Comons the seyd tyme,
aft̃ ijd. ob yᵉ day . . . . . .    ijs. vjd.

Itm̃ to yᵉ Mason yᵉ iijᵗʰ tyme for v dayes, aft̃ vjd. yᵉ
day . . . . . . . . . .    ijs. vjd.

Itm̃ to hys Juant for yᵉ seyd tyme, aft̃ iijd. the day .    xvd.

Itm̃ payed to my selfe for yᵉʳ Comōs yᵉ seyd tyme, aft̃
ijd. ob yᵉ day . . . . . . . .    ijs. jd.

Itm̃ to yᵉ Mason yᵉ iiijᵗʰ tyme for v dayes, aft̃ vjd. the
day . . . . . . . . . .    ijs. vjd.

Itm̃ to hys Man yᵉ seyd tyme, aft̃ iijd. yᵉ daye . .    xvd.

Itm̃ Alowed to my selfe for yᵉʳ Coms̃ yᵉ seyd tyme, aft̃
ijd. ob yᵉ day . . . . . . . .    ijs. jd.

D

Itm̃ Alowed to yᵉ Mason for Symond .   .   .   .      iiij*d.*

Itm̃ to Tylney for yᵉ Mendyng of Certen glasse⎫
wyndowes wᵗin yᵉ Chyrche of Northelmhm̃ .   .⎭   ij*s.*

Itm̃ payed to Thom̃s Shetell for yᵉ Caryeng of ij lodes⎫
of Grauell ℈ one loud of Sande .   .   .   .⎭   ix*d.*

Aᵒ dm. 1542ᵒ.

Aᵒ Dm.
1542.

The Receyts of me, Thom̃s powle aforseyd, the other Chyrchewarden.

In p⁹imis reč of yᵉ town at the Acompts .   .   .    xx*s.*

Itm̃ reč of Robt Rudd of Betele for lond ferme .   .   xxv*s.*

Itm̃ reč of yarrhm̃ men for yᵉ bryngyng of yᵉ lytle⎫
bell from Norwyche .   .   .   .   .   .⎭   xiiij*d.*

The wholl sum̃e of yᵉ Receyts of me, Thom̃s powle⎫
aforseyd   .   .   .   .   .   .   .⎭   ys xlvj*s.*   ij*d.*

These be yᵉ Expenss and Charges leyd owte by me yᵉ seyd Thom̃s
powle ℈ one of yᵉ Chyrchewardens of Northelmhm̃ yᵉ yere of
oʳ lord god aforeseyd, ℈c.

In p⁹imis Alowed to my selue for yᵉ Comons of Alyn ℈⎫
hys sone iiij dayes, aft̃ ij*d.* oᵬ yᵉ day for yche⎬   xx*d.*
of them .   .   .   .   .   .   .⎭

Itm̃ to Jooãne patrycke for makyng clean of Seynt⎫
Johns Chapell .   .   .   .   .   .⎭   j*d.*

Itm̃ to John Mayor for makyng clean yᵉ Steyers of⎫
yᵉ Steple .   .   .   .   .   .⎭   j*d.*

Itm̃ for A Horse wyche the Mason had to ryde wᵗ to⎫
Walsynghm̃ whan yᵉ fre Stone was bought .   .⎭   ij*d.*

Itm̃ payed to Alyn yᵉ belhanger vpon Halowmes euyn,⎫
yn yᵉ yere aforseyd, ℈ for my pte .   .   .⎭   vj*s.*   viij*d.*

Itm̃ payed to yᵉ Smythe for makyng ℈ trymyng of⎫
℈rten yrons for yᵉ bells ℈ yn pte of A more Sum̃e⎭   xx*d.*

Itm̄ payed to Alyn yᵉ bell hanger Another tyme,⎫
wyche was vpon yᵉ fryday next before Seynt⎬ iijˢ. iiijᵈ.
Luke, yn yᵉ yere of owʳ lorde god aforseyd . .⎭

Itm̄ to yᶜ Smythe Another tyme for suche thyngs as⎫ iijˢ. ijᵈ.
was occupyed Abowte the bells . . . .⎭

Itm̄ payed for lether for yᵉ baderycke for yᶜ lytle bell . vjᵈ.

Itm̄ payed to m̄ dythycke for yᵉ lete fee⁽²⁵⁾ of⎫
Northelmhm̄ . . . . . . .⎬ xxiiijˢ.

Itm̄ to Mʳᵉˢ dythycke for gressc for yᵉ seyd bells . . jᵈ.

Itm̄ for yᵉ Comons of Alyn ₴ hys sone iiij dayes, aft̄⎫ xxᵈ.
ijᵈ. oƀ yᵉ day . . . . . . .⎭

Sum̄, xixˢ. jᵈ. ₴ xxiiijᵗʰˢ.

the sum̄e of yᵉ Reč of me Thom̄s powlle aforseyd ys . xlvjˢ. ijᵈ.

the sum̄e of yᵉ Expenss ₴ Chargs of me yᶜ seyd Tho.⎫ xliijˢ. jᵈ.
powle ys . . . . . . . .⎭

And so remayn yn yᵉ hands of me yᵉ seyd Thom̄s⎫
powlc, As ys here leyd down at yᶜ Acompts yn⎬ iijˢ. jᵈ.
mony . . . . . . . . .⎭

And so yᵉ seyd Thom̄s powle ys dyscharged for thys yere.

Mᵈ. aft̄ yᵉ Rekenyng made Thom̄s powle hathe Chosen to be hys
felow for thys Comyng Wyllm̄ Thomsñ, husbondman.
Deliu⁹id them yn hand . viijˢ.

S. (scilicet) to Thom̄s powle iiijˢ. And to Wyllm̄ Thompsñ iiijˢ.

Aº dın. 1543º.

Mᵈ. A Rekenyng made the Wedn⁹seday yn Wyghtson Weke yᵉ yere
of oʳ Lord god ᴍˡˡ ccccc xliijᵗⁱ of Thom̄s powle And Wyllm̄
Thompson, Husbondman, Chyrchwardens of Northelmhm̄.
The Reč of vs yᵉ forseyd Thom̄s And Wyllm̄.

In p⁹imis Reč at yᵉ Accompts . . . . . viijˢ.

Itm̃ for A pursse & ij Combs yᵗ were Relyquys in yᵉ ⎫
Chyrche ⁽²⁶⁾ . . . . . . . .⎭ iijs.

Itm̃ for Halowmes nyght all thyngs dyscharged due at ⎫
yᵗ tyme . . . . . . . .⎭ ijs. ijd.

Itm̃ reč of Thoñs Shetell for lond fferme . . . iiijs. xd.

Itm̃ reč of Nycholas purdy for lond fferme . . . xvjd.

Itm̃ reč of Wyllm̃ lussher for lond fferme, ijs., & yᵉ ⎫
Campynclosse, ijs. . . . . . .⎭ iiijs.

Itm̃ reč of wyllm̃ ffranckelyng for londe fferme . . xijd.

Itm̃ reč of Jaffry Rudd for lond fferme . . . xd.

Itm̃ reč of Wyllm̃ yarrhm̃ for lond fferme . . . ijs.

Itm̃ reč of Wyllm̃ Rudd for yᵉ wodd yᵗ grew (in) yᵉ ⎫
Campyngclosse dytche . . . . . .⎭ xvs.

Itm̃ reč of Herry Rustñ for lond fferme . . . ijs.

Itm̃ reč of Robt Rudd of Betele, for lond fferme ⎫
lyeng yᵉʳ . . . . . . . .⎭ xxvs.

Itm̃ reč of Mʳᵉˢ dethyke for lond fferme yᵉʳ, aft̃ vjd. yᵉ ⎫
Acr⁹ . . . . . . . . .⎭ vs. vjd.

Itm̃ reč of Robt Sohm̃ for londe fferme yᵉʳ . . ijs.

Itm̃ reč of Rychard Crow for lond fferme yᵉʳ . . ijs. viijd.

Itm̃ of Thoñs Howsse for lond fferme ther . . vjs.

Itm̃ reč of same Thoñs Howse for yᵉ laste yers fferme. ijs.

Total Suñã reč, iiijli. vijs. iiijd.

These be yᵉ Expenss & Chargs leyd owte by the seyd Thoñs Powle
& Wyllm̃ Thompson the ycre of oʳ lord god Aforseyd, &c.

In p⁹imis to yᵉ iiij men yn to yᵉ kyngs worcks at Gyens xvjd.

Itm̃ to yᵉ breke borners of How for ij C Tyle for ⎫
yᵉ Chyrche . . . . . . . .⎭ iijs. iiijd.

Itm̃ to Wyllm̃ Chambyrlyn for ij keyes for ij Chests in ⎫
yᵉ Chyrche . . . . . . . .⎭ viijd.

Itm̃ to yᵉ seyd Wyllm̃ for A bolte for yᵉ grett bell & }
for other yrons & Nayles for yᵉ seyd bell . . } xxd.

Itm̃ to lussher & Cursñ for makyng of yᵉ Town butts ⁽²⁷⁾ xijd.

Redd ͭ. Itm̃ to yᵉ Coller of Elmhm̃ for yᵉ Rent of yᵉ Town londs vijs.

Itm̃ m̃ dethyke for yᵒ lete ffee . . . . . xxiiijs.

Itm̃ to John Gogney for yᵉ halfe yere Rent of Betele . ijs. vjd.

Itm̃ to m̃ dethyke for An Acr⁹ of offyce lond . . vijd.

Itm̃ to Rycharde Crow for yᵉ Rent of A Medow in Betele vjd.

Sum̃, xlijs. vijd.

Itm̃ to Robt Rudd of Betele for yᵉ Taxe yᵉʳ . . vs.

Itm̃ to Wyllm̃ Smythe for yᵉ fynysshyng of the dytche }
of Northelmhm̃ Comon at yᵉ Este pte of yᵉ hethe. } ijs.

Itm̃ to A Mason iij dayes for pauyng of yᵉ Chyrche . xijd.

Itm̃ to hym for hys sones wags yᵉ seyd iij dayes . . vjd.

Itm̃ for ther Comons the seyd iij dayes . . . xijd.

Itm̃ for vj bʒ of lyme, ixd., & to Robt Rud of Betele }
for yᵉ bryngyng home of yt from Walsynghm̃ . } xiijd.

Itm̃ to lyngeyes wyffe for makyng clen of yᵉ Chyrche }
aft̃ yᵉ Masons . . . . . . . } ijd.

Itm̃ for lether for yᵒ lytell bell badrycke . . . ijd.

Itm̃ to one yͭ went to bye yᵉ seyd lyme at Walsynghm̃ ijd.

Itm̃ leyd owte towarde yᵉ Taxe of Northelmhm̃ . . iiijs.

Itm̃ payed for yᵉ makyng of vij Combs of Malte . . xxjd.

Itm̃ to Thom̃s Shetell for yᵉ Caryeng of one lode of }
Sande whan the Chyrche was paued . . . } iijd.

Itm̃ to Mʳᵉˢ dethyke for Nayles occupyed at Chyrche . jd.

Itm̃ to Handforthe for yᵉ bryngyng home of vjli. of }
waxe frō Norwyche for the Comon lyghte . . } jd.

Itm̃ to Wyllm̃ Smythe for yᵉ hedgyng of the ynward }
pte of yᵉ Campyng Closse dytche . . . } xijd.

Itm̃ for y⁰ offeryng ҁ waxe at y⁰ obytee day of y⁰  }  ijd.
bñfactors [28] . . . . . . . . . }

Itm̃ payed for y⁰ Caryeng of ij hūdered Tyles for to }  vjd.
paue wᵗ all y⁰ Chyrche at Elmhm̃ from How . }

Itm̃ for A Tubb wyche y⁰ Masons had at Chyrche  }
bothc y⁰ laste yere and this. And was fayn to be  }  iiijd.
hoped at bothe tymes . . . . . . }

Itm̃ payed to John wodcoke y⁰ elder for pte of y⁰ ferme  }
of ᵃrten londs lyeng yn the ffoulde Course of  }
Northelmhm̃, wyche y⁰ Townchype heyred of hym  }
y⁰ʳ iijs. vjd. And y⁰ reste, wyche ys xvjs., in full  }
paymēt for y⁰ fferme of y⁰ seyd londs frō yere to  }  iijs. vjd.
yere, so longe As he ys ffermer As ys Agred  }
betwen y⁰ seyd Townchype ҁ hym, was payed  }
by the hands of Nycholas dyght ҁ other of y⁰  }
same Town, wyche As now hathe y⁰ seyd londs yn  }
fearme . . . . . . . . }

Sum̃, xxijs. ixd.

The Sum̃e of y⁰ Reč of y⁰ seyd Thom̃s ҁ Wyllm̃ ys   iiijli. vijs. iiijd.

The Sum̃e of y⁰ Expēss ҁ Chargs of y⁰ seyd Tho. ҁ  }  iijli. vs. iiijd.
Wy. ys . . . . . . . . . }

And so remayn in ther hands As ys here leyd down yn  }  xxijs.
Monye at y⁰ʳ Accompts . . . . . }

Et sic quieti And so y⁰ seyd Thom̃s powle ҁ Wyllm̃ Thompson be clerly dys-
sñt dicti charged for this yere paste.
Thom̃s ҁ
Willm̃9pro Mᵈ. Aft̶ y⁰ Rekenyng made Wyllm̃ Thomsñ hathe chosen to be hys
hoc Anno ffelow for thys yere Comyng Wyllm̃ ffrankelynge. Delyuᵖed
predicto. them yn hande. s. to y⁰ seyd Wyllm̃ Thompsñ ҁ Wyllm̃
ffrankelyng.

A° Dm.
1544.
[A° 36°
Hen.VIII.]

A° dm. 1544°.

M⁴. A Rekenyng made yᵉ Wedn⁹sedaye in Whyghtsonweke yᵉ yere of owʳ Lorde god ᴍ¹ᶜᶜᶜᶜ ꝛ xliiijᵗⁱ of Wyllm̄ Thompson ꝛ Wyllm̄ ffranckelynge, Chyrchewardens of Northelmhm̄.

The rec̃ of vs yᵉ forseyd Wyllm̄ ꝛ Wyllm̄.

In p⁹imis receyued at yᵉ Accompts as ys Aforseyd . xxˢ.

Itm̄ rec̃ of Mʳᵉˢ dethyke for yᵉ quethode of hyr Husbonde, gyffne by hys Testamēt to yᵉ repacōn of } xxˢ.
yˢ Chyrche yᵉʳ . . . . . . . .

Itm̄ rec̃ of M⁹ Nycholls for pcell of yᵉ quethode
gyffne by the Testamēt of M⁹ Sylues꟱, late
Vycar of Elmhm̄, towarde yᵉ Repācōn of yᵉ
noysome wayes yᵉʳ to be bestowed At owʳ dys- } xˢ. viijⅆ.
crecōn, xˢ. viijⅆ., ꝛ how yᵉ Rest was bestowed yt
ys playnly set forthe in yᵉ latter ende of thys
boke . . . . . . . . .

(Mʳ Sylvester's "quethode"—end of the book. A° dm. 1543°).

M⁴. yᵗ these be yᵉ Sum̄es of mony payed by M⁹ Robt Nycholls,[29] psn of Raynhm̄ Margaret, And Executor of yᵉ Testamēt And Laste Wyll of M⁹ Syluester, late Vycar of Northelmhm̄, towarde yᵉ mendyng of yᵉ noysome wayes [30] ther, Acordyng to yᵉ Testamēt ꝛ Laste Wyll of yᵉ seyd M⁹ Syluester the yere of owʳ Lorde ᴍ¹ⁱcccccxliijᵗⁱ payeng to eu⁹y man for hym selfe hys Horses, Carte, Comons, ꝛ Wags, af꟱ xijⅆ. yᵉ daye, by the space of iij dayes. And to eu⁹y laborer yᵉ seyd dayes for yᵉʳ Wags ꝛ Comons af꟱ vⅆ. yᵉ daye yf they were good ꝛ suffycyēt laborers. And vnto meane laborers af꟱ iiijⅆ. yᵉ day for yᵉʳ Wags ẕ Comons. And vnto ladds aft̃ iijd. yᵉ day. As hereaft̃ more playnly shall Apere in seuᵛall pcells. Wrytten by s̃ John Eluᵛyche, pysshe p̃ʸyste yᵉʳ the yere ẕ tyme Afore exp̃ssid.

### To yᵉ Caryers yᵉ fyrste daye.

| | |
|---|---|
| In p̃ʸimis to Nycholas dyght, xvjd. To Rychard Watson, xvjd. | ijs. viijd. |
| Itm̃ to Wyllm̃ Wakefelde, xvjd. To Stephen Loue, xvjd. | ijs. viijd. |
| Itm̃ to Wyllm̃ dyxe, xvjd. To Wyllm̃ Tylney, xvjd. | ijs. viijd. |
| Itm̃ to Thom̃s Lussher, xvjd. To Rycharde Man, xvjd. | ijs. viijd. |
| Itm̃ to Nycholas Purdye, xvjd. To Rycharde Purdy, xvjd. | ijs. viijd. |
| Itm̃ to Rycharde Hey, At yᵉ Crosse (31), xvjd. To Wyllm̃ yarhm̃, xvjd. | ijs. viijd. |
| Itm̃ to Wyllm̃ Rudd, xvjd. To Thom̃s Shetell, xvjd. | ijs. viiid. |

### To yᵉ laborers yᵉ same daye.

| | |
|---|---|
| In p̃ʸimis to Thom̃s Cursñ, vd. To John Brese, vd. To Robt Lyngey, vd. | xvd. |
| Itm̃ to Robt Reymer, vd. To Willm̃ dyxe, vd. To Willm̃ Smythe, vd. | xvd. |
| Itm̃ to Thom̃s powle, vd. Thom̃s Blackbᵛro, vd. To Ry. Robynsñ, vd. | xvd. |
| Itm̃ to John Mayer, iiijd. To Herry Lussher, vd. To Rycharde Purdye, vd. | xiiijd. |
| Itm̃ to Jaffry Rudde, vd. Thom̃s patrycke, vd. Wyllm̃ Wylsñ, vd. | xvd. |
| Itm̃ to Herry Wells, vd. Loues Ladde, iijd. Tylneyes Ladde, iijd. Reyners Ladde, iijd. | xiiijd. |

Itm̃ to dyghts Ladde, iijd. Purdyes Ladde, iijd. Herry ⎫
Wakefelde, iijd. Thompsñs Ladde, iijd. . .⎭ xijd.

The Suñie of yᵉ mony payed to yᵉ Caʳyers and ⎫
Laborers yᵉ fyrste daye ys. . . .⎭ xxvijs.

## To yᵉ Caryers yᵉ seconde daye.

In pⁱimis to Thoñis Shetell, xvjd.; Wyllñ yarrhñ, ⎫
xvjd. . . . . . . . . .⎭ ijs. viijd.

Itm̃ to Symon Shetell, xvjd.; Ry. Heywarde at yᵉ ⎫
Crosse, xvjd. . . . . . .⎭ ijs. viijd.

Itm̃ to Nycholas Purdy, xvjd.; Wyllñ dyxe, xvjd.; ⎫
Ny. dyght, xvjd. . . . . . .⎭ iiijs.

Itm̃ to Wyllñ Rudde for d. A daye, viijd.; Rycharde ⎫
Heywarde the elder for A Carte ⁊ A Horsse, vjd.; ⎬ ijs. vjd.
Rycharde Man, xvjd. . . . . .⎭

Itm̃ to Stephen Loue for A Carte ⁊ A Horsse . . vjd.

## To yᵉ Laborers yᵉ same daye.

In pⁱimis Robt Worchope, vd.; Thoñis Clercke, ij dayes, ⎫
xd.; John Brese, vd. . . . . . .⎭ xxd.

Itm̃ Wyllñ Wyllsñ, vd.; Robt Reyner, vd.; Thoñis ⎫
Cursñ, vd.; Wy. Smythe, vd. . . . .⎭ xxd.

Itm̃ to Andrew Wakefelde, ij days, xd.; Rycharde Purdy, ⎫
vd.; Stephñ Loue, vd. . . . . . .⎭ xxd.

Itm̃ to Wy. Thōpsñ, laborer, vd.; Wyllñ Lussher, iiijd.; ⎫
Thoñis Shetell, vd. . . . . . .⎭ xiiijd.

Itm̃ to Bertylmew Stephensñ, vd.; Wyllñ dyxe, vd.; ⎫
Wyllñ Thōpsñ, vd. . . . . . .⎭ xvd.

Itm̃ to Rycharde Heywarde at yᵉ oke, yᵉ owʳ seer of yᵉ ⎫
Laborers . . . . . . . .⎭ viijd.

Itm̃ to Shetells Ladde, ij dayes, vjd.; Syzons Ladde,  
iiijd.; Rudds Ladde, ij dayes, vd. . . . . — xvd.

Itm̃ to Tylneyes Ladde, ijd. ; Reyners Ladde, ijd.;  
dyghts Ladde, ijd.; yarrhm̃s Ladde, ij dayes, iiijd. . — xd.

Itm̃ to Rycharde Heywards Ladde for ij days . . — vd.

Itm̃ in Expenss the ij dayes Afore exp⁹ssid for hys selfe,  
his Horses, hys s⁹uant, & dy⁹use other of yᵉ Town — iijs. iiijd.

The Sum̃e of yᵉ mony payed to yᵉ Caryers &  
Laberers yᵉ ij day ys xxiijs. And yᵉ Expenss  
the seyd ij dayes, As ys Afore specyfyed, ys — xxvjs. iiijd.  
iijs. iiijd. . . . . . . .

To yᵉ Caryers yᵉ iijᵗʰ daye.

In p⁹imis to Ry. Heywarde yᵉ elder, xvjd., Thom̃s  
Shetell, xvjd. . . . . . . . — ijs. viijd.

Itm̃ to Ry. Heywarde At yᵉ Crosse, xvjd.; Rycharde  
Purdye, xvjd. . . . . . . . — ijs. viijd.

Itm̃ to Wyllm̃ Thompsoñ, xvjd.; John Wodcocke, xvjd. — ijs. viijd.

To yᵉ Laborers yᵉ same daye.

In p⁹imis to Thom̃s Shetell, vd.; Roᵬt Worckepe, vd.;  
Wyllm̃ Here, vd. . . . . . . — xvd.

Itm̃ to Bertyllmew Stephësñ, vd.; Wyllm̃ Thompsñ,  
vd.; Roᵬt Reyner, vd. . . . . . — xvd.

Itm̃ to Thom̃s Cursñ, vd.; Stephen Loue, vd.; Wyllm̃  
Smythe, vd. . . . . . . . — xvd.

Itm̃ to Rycharde Heywarde, vd.; Thom̃s Clarcke, ijd.;  
Wy. Wylsñ, ijd. . . . . . . — ixd.

Itm̃ to Thom̃s Stephësñ, ijd.; to iij yᵗ brake yᵉʳ Carte  
Axelltres, vjd. . . . . . . . — viijd.

Itm̃ to Wyllm̃ Rudd, xvj*d*., in Expenss y*e* same day, xij*d*.; to vj Ladds, vj*d*. . . . . . — ij*s*. x*d*.

Itm̃ delyu⁹d to y*e* Chyrche Wardens, s. Wyllm̃ ffrāckelyng & Wyllm̃ Thompsñ, x*s*. viij*d*., to be-stoue yt wher As they thyncke moste meate & cōuenyc̃t aft̃ y*er* dyscrecōn . . . . . — x*s*. viij*d*.

The Sum̃e of mony payed to y*e* Caryers & Laborers y*e* iij*th* daye ys xv*s*., & y*e* sum̃e of Expenss y*e* same daye ys xij*d*., & y*e* Sum̃o of y*e* mony that was delyu⁹d to y*e* Chyrche Wardens, s. Wyllm̃ ffrancke-lyng & Wyllm̃ Thōpsñ ys x*s*. viij*d*. . . . — xxvj*s*. viij*d*.

Sum̃a Total p⁹cedens, iiijli.

A° Dm̃ 1544 (continued).

Itm̃ rec̃ for y*e* quethode of Thom̃s Heywarde, late of Gatele . . . . . . . . — ij*s*.

Itm̃ rec̃ of Wyllm̃ yarrhm̃ & John Brese, w*t* y*e* Consent of dyu⁹se of the Inhabytañce y*er* for y*e* grante of y*e* Town Closse lyeng w*t*in Betele, to hold to them & y*er* assignes xv yers, v*s*. for An yncomyng besyds y*e* yerly ferme, y*e* seyd tyme wyche shalbe yerly xx*s*. . . . . . . . . — v*s*.

Itm̃ rec̃ for y*e* pfyghts of Halowmes nyght all thyngs due at tyme dyscharged . . . . . — ij*s*. x*d*.

Itm̃ rec̃ for vj Comb; of malte & j b;, Alowyng for y*e* Caryeng to y*e* Kyngs Myll *(32)* & so furthe to Twyforde to y*e* Beare bruars, vj*d*. . . . — xij*s*.

Itm̃ rec̃ for pte of y*e* fferme londs w*t*in Northelmhm̃ . — xv*s*.

Itm̃ rec̃ for pte of y*e* fferme londs, Betele . . . xxxv*s*. ij*d*.

Sum̃a Totali (sic) p⁹cedens rec̃, vjli. ij*s*. viij*d*.

These be yᵉ Expenss ᵵ Chargs leyd owte by the seyd Wyllm̄ ffrankelyng ᵵ Wyllm̄ Thompsñ, yᵉ yere of oʳ Lorde god Aforseyd.

In pᵒimis to wyllm̄ Smythe for fellyng of thornes ᵵ }
hedgyng of yᵒ Est syde of the Campyng Closse . } xxd.

Itm̄ to Edm̄ñde Ram for ye caryeng of yᵉ seyd thornes xxd.

Itm̄ to John Lamberde for A falde gate to hange at yᵉ }
Hethe, And for hoks, hengells, wᵗ other yrons for } xxjd.
yᵉ seyd gate . . . . . . . . }

Itm̄ to Reynher for dyggyng of Grauell for yᵉ wayc }
At yᵉ Hethe iij dayes; for hys wages, Meate, ᵵ } xvd.
drynke . . . . . . . . . }

Itm̄ to Cursñ yᵉ seyd iij dayes yᵉʳ xvd., ᵵ to Wyllm̄ }
Smythe yᵉ seyd tyme, xvd. . . . . . } ijs. vjd.

Itm̄ to Rychard Watson for one day wᵗ hys Carte ᵵ ij }
dayes worcke of hym selffe ther . . . . } xxijd.

Itm̄ to Nycholas dyght for one daye ᵵ d. wᵗ hys Carte, }
And for A plancke to ley oū the grope at the } ijs. ijd.
Hethe . . . . . . . . . }

Itm̄ to Robt Lussher for A dayes worcke ther . . vd.

Itm̄ for nayles for yᵉ bells ᵵ dyuᵒse other thyngs yᵉʳ . ob

Itm̄ to wryght for the makyng of yᵒ lytell bell Clapper, }
And for mendyng of yᵉ thyrd bell Clapper . . } iijs.

Itm̄ payed to yᵉ bekon watche, for yᵉ offeryng at Mᵖ }
Smythes obyte . . . . . . . } iiijs. jd.

Itm̄ payed to Mᵖ Martyns sᵖuant for yᵉ Rent of one }
Rode of londe in the hands of Wyllm̄ ffranckelyng } jd.

Itm̄ in Expenss whan I rode to Geyghton⁽⁸³⁾ for yᵉ }
Townes busynes by the Commandemēt of yᵉ }
Comyssary yᵉʳ for serten maters towchyng sᵖrten } vijd.
godly requests of owʳ souᵖayn lorde yᵒ kyng . }

Itm̃ to wyllm̃ yarrhm̃ for mendyng of yᵉ pulpytt for oʳ ⎫
pte . . . . . . . . . ⎭    viijd.

Itm̃ to Wyllm̃ Tylney for yᵉ mendyng of Glase ⎫
wyndow vpon the sougthe syde of the Chyrche . ⎭    viijd.

Itm̃ payed to yᵉ balye of yᵉ hundered for yᵉ bekon ⎫
watche . . . . . . . . . ⎭    ijs.

Itm̃ payed to my lady hastens balye for the Rent of A ⎫
medow lyeng in Bytteryng . . . . . ⎭    vjd.

Itm̃ to yᵉ Constables of Gressenhall for yᵉ taxe of yᵉ ⎫
seyd medow . . . . . . . . ⎭    vjd.

Sum̃, xxvs. iiijd. ob.


Itm̃ to yᵉ Constables of Betele for yᵉ taxe of owʳ ⎫
londs yᵉʳ . . . . . . . . ⎭    vs.

Itm̃ in Expenss at lytchm̃ whan we were ther At yᵉ ⎫
generall by the Commandemēt of Mᴰ heythe yᵉ ⎬    vijd.
Comyssary generall than . . . . . ⎭

Itm̃ to yᵉ forseyd baly of this hūdered for yᵉ bekon ⎫
watche . . . . . . . . . ⎭    xijd.

Itm̃ payed towarde yᵉ taxe of Northelmhm̃ . . . xijs. iiijd.

Itm̃ to herry ffylde & hys Compenye for pte of dytchyng ⎫
for sᵉrten of owʳ londs lyeng wᵗin Betele . . ⎭    xs.

Reddᵗ    Itm̃ to yᵉ Colour of Northelmhm̃ for yᵉ Rente of yᵉ ⎫
londs yᵉʳ . . . . . . . . ⎭    vijs.

Itm̃ to the baly ther for yᵉ lete ffe . . . . xxiiijs.

Itm̃ to hym for yᵉ Rente of owʳ londs lyeng wᵗin Betele    vs.

Itm̃ to yᵉ forseyd Herry ffylde & his Compenye for pte ⎫
of dytchyng of sᵉrten of owʳ londs lyeng wᵗin ⎬    xijs. viijd.
Betele . . . . . . . . . ⎭

Itm̃ to Joħn Wodcocke for pte of yᵉ fferme of serten ⎱   iijₛ.   vjᵈ.
londs lyeng w'in the fowlde Course of Northelmhm̃ ⎰

             Sum̃, iiijₗᵢ. xiijᵈ.

Itm̃ Alowed to my selffe for caryeng of Grauell ⅋⎫
dyggyng of yᵉ same ij dayes vnto byllyngforde ⎪
brydge, ⅋ to yᵉ lane also of the bake syde of ⎬ iijₛ. viijᵈ.
olde Shetells, ⅋ for meate, drynke, ⅋ wags for ⎪
my selffe ⅋ my s⁹uants the seyd time . . .⎭

            Sum̃ Totali *(sic)* Solut⁹, vₗᵢ. ixₛ. jᵈ. ob̃.

The Sum̃e of yᵉ Rec̃ of yᵉ seyd Wyllm̃ ⅋ Wyllm̃ ys    . vjₗᵢ. ijₛ. viijᵈ.
The Sum̃e of yᵉ Expess ⅋ Chargs of yᵉ seyd Wy. ⅋ Wy. ys vₗᵢ. ixₛ. jᵈ. ob̃.
And so remayn in yᵉʳ hands As ys here leyd down in ⎱ xiijₛ. vjᵈ. ob̃.
monye at ther Accompts   .   .   .   .   . ⎰

**Et sic qui-**
**eti sñt dicti**
**Willm̃9 ⅋**
**Willm̃9 p**
**hoc Anno**
**p⁹dicto.**

And so the seyd Wyllm̃ Thompsñ ⅋ Wyllm̃ ffrankelyng be clerly
dyscharged for yˡˢ yere paste.

Mᵈ. After yᵉ Rekenyng made Wyllm̃ ffranckelyng hathe chosen to
be his felow for this yere comyng Edmunde ffletcher.

Delyu⁹id yᵉᵐ in hande, that ys to seye, to yᵉ seyd ⎱ xjₛ.   ijᵈ.
Wyllm̃ ffranckelyng ⅋ Edmñde ffletcher   .   .⎰

**Aᵒ Dm.**
**1545.**
**[Aᵒ 37ᵒ**
**Hen. VIII.]**

         Aᵒ dm̃ 1545ᵒ.

Mᵈ. A Rekenyng made yᵉ Wedn⁹sedaye in Whyghtsonweke the yᵉʳᵉ
of owʳ lorde god Mˡˡccccc ⅋ xlvᵗˡ of Wyllm̃ fråkelyng ⅋ Edmñde
ffletcher, Chyrchwardens of Northelmhm̃, ⅋c.

     The Receyts of us, yᵉ foreseyd Willm̃ ⅋ Edmñde ffletcher.

In p⁹imis Receyuid At yᵉ Accompts As ys Afore ⎱ xjₛ.   ijᵈ.
specyfyed   .   .   .   .   .   .   .   . ⎰

Itm̃ rec̃ of John Gogneye for yᵉ quethode of his father ⎱ xxₛ.
to yᵉ Chyrche   .   .   .     .   . ⎰

furres solu⁹  Itm̄ reċ of Warner of Gatele for s̓rten ffurres yᵗ he ⎱  ijd.
ı.e., soluti      had vpon yᵉ Comon  .  .  .  .  .  ⎰

ı.unt, have  Itm̄ reċ of Wyllm̄ Thompsñ for yᵉ olde dett of ⎫
ıeen paid      Thow̄se (sic) Howse of Betele for A Closse ȥ ⎬  iijs. viijd.
ıor).          other londs lyeng ther  .  .  .  .  .  ⎭

Itm̄ reċ of yᵉ pson of Bylney (34) for s̓rten londs lyeng ⎱  xs. viijd.
w̓in yᵉ bownds of Betele, leyng now ynclosed  . ⎰

It reċ of Jhon Hall for yᵒ fferme of s̓rten londs ther  .   ijs.

Itm̄ reċ of Wyllm̄ yarrhm̄ for yᵉ Towne Closse lyeng ⎫
in Betele, xxs., ȥ for s̓rten londs lyeing w̓in ⎬ xxijs.
Elmhm̄, ijs. .  .  .  .  .  .  .  . ⎭

Itm̄ reċ of Thom̄s Shetell for londe ferme in Elmhm̄  .   iiijs.   xd.

Itm̄ reċ of Thom̄s lussher for londe ferme w̓in North- ⎫
elmhm̄, ijs., ȥ of hym reċ for yᵉ Campyng ⎬ iiijs.
closse, ijs. .  .  .  .  .  .  .  . ⎭

Itm̄ reċ of Robt Rudd for s̓rten of yᵉ Town londs ⎱  ixs.   vjd.
lyeng w̓in Betele, by heryngs now ynclosed  . ⎰

Itm̄ reċ of yᵉ pfyghts for halowmes nyght, besyds all ⎫
thyngs dyscharged due to be payed at yᵗ tyme, as ⎪
for yᵒ wasshyng of yᵉ Syrples, tendyng yᵒ bells, ȥ ⎪
such other ; ȥ also payed Afore hande for iiij bȝ of ⎬ ijs.
Malte Ageynst yᵒ next yᵉʳᵉ, wyche shall be payed ⎪
ȥ delyu⁹id by Wyllm̄ dycke or his Assignes w̓ A ⎪
heape at yᵉ Combȝ, ȥc. .  .  .  .  .  . ⎭

Itm̄ reċ of Rychard Crow for yᵉ ferme of A Medow  .   ijs. viijd.

Itm̄ reċ of John Rudd of Betele for Thornes owte of ⎱  viijd.
yᵉ owʳ Closse yᵉʳ  .  .  .  .  .  .  . ⎰

Itm̄ receyuid of Jaffry Rudd for londe fferme  .  .   xd.

Itm̄ reċ of Nycholas purdy for londe fferme.  .  .   xvjd.

Sum̄a Total p̓cedens reċ, iiijli. xiiijs. ijd. ȥ xvjd.

These be yᵉ Expenss & Charges leyd owte by the sᵈ Wyllm̃ ffranckelyng
& Edmñde ffletcher yᵉ yere of oʳ lord god Aforseyd, &c.

In pᵉimis to Wyllm̃ Tylney, vjs. viijd. in pte of paymẽt
of xxs. for yᵉ taken down of yᵉ panes of euᵖy
wyndow of ye Clery Storyes, & muste surely &
Substancyally make & Amende yᵉᵐ wᵗ all yᵉ other
wyndowes also yᵗ be now perysshed, & pmysed to
do yᵉᵐ betwyxe yᵉ Rekenyng at Wyghtsondaye,
yᵉ yere of owʳ lorde Aforseyd, & Mychaelmes next ⎱ vjs.   viijd.
aft̃ yᵗ. And furder he bynde hym selffe by thys ⎰
pᵉsens to yᵉ seyd Chyrchwardens yᵉʳ, & also other
succedyng yᵉᵐ from tyme to tyme beyng, yᵗ he
shall Substancyally kepe yᵉ seyd wyndowes of yᵉ
Clerye Storyes duryng hys lyffe naturall at his
own xpse, Coste, & charge, for xijd. yᵉ yere,
&c.  .   .   .   .   .   .   .   .

Itm̃ payede to yᵉ seyd Wyllm̃ Tylneye At tweyn
seuerall tymes aft̃ that in full Contentacõn &
paymẽt of yᵉ seyd xxs. for yᵉ taken down & ⎬ xiijs.  iiijd.
mendyng of yᵉ seyd wyndowes of yᵒ Clery Storyes
& other in maꝶ & forme Aforseyd.  .   .

Itm̃ payed to Herry ffylde for sellyng of Thornes for
yᵉ new closse lyeng by Heryngs in Betele, xxd., &
to Edmñde Ram, Stephen Loue, for Caryeng of
Thornes ij dayes to yᵉ seyd Closse, iiijs. viijd., ⎬ viijs.  xd.
payed Also to yᵉ seyd Herry ffylde And Rycharde
Robyns, for hedgyng of yᵉ seyd Closse, ijs. vjd.

Itm̃ payed for A syde of lether for yᵉ bawedrecks of yᵉ
bells, xviijd., & to John Wryght for A ffyer pañe ⎱ vs.  iiijd.
& A buckell for A badrycke, xd.; & to hym for ⎰
yᵉ mendyng of ij bell Clappers, iijs.  .   .

Itm̃ payed to yᵉ lords Colour of yˡˢ maﬁ for yᵉ leate ffe,⎫
xxiiijs.; ₴ for ij payer of botes for yᵉ Soydyors yᵗ ⎪ **xxxs. viijd.**
sholde haue gone furthe ⁽³⁵⁾ yᵉ yere that ys paste, ⎪
₴c., vjs. viijd. . . . . . . ⎭

Sum̃, iijli. iiijs. xd.

ᴸaddiᵗ solᵞ  Itm̃ to Blackebrow for A Ratchett ⁽³⁶⁾ xxd.; for yᵉ Rent⎫
i.e. Reditus  of yᵉ town londs, vijs.; for yᵉ rent of yᵉ town⎪
ᵢₒlutus est,  londs lyeng in Betele, vs.; ₴ for yᵉ town londs⎬ **xiiijs. ijd.**
ᴸerent has  holde of my lady hastyngs, vjd. . . . ⎭
ᵤen paid).  Itm̃ to one Sawnder of yᵉ same town for A Swerd ₴⎫
A daggarde for one of yᵉ Soydyors yᵗ shold haue⎬ **ijs. viijd.**
gone furthe . . . . . . . . ⎭

Itm̃ to Roger Hamonde for ffellyng of An ocke in yᵉ⎫
pcke for yᵉ mendyng of yᵉ brydge by Rudds, iijd.;⎪
to ffyncke for yᵉ glasyng of iij panes of A wyndow⎬ **vs.**
in Seynt James Chapell, iiijs. vjd.; for iij Gyrdles⎪
for yᵉ Albes,⁽³⁷⁾ iijd. . . . . . . ⎭

Itm̃ to John Wryght for yᵉ makyng of v new barres⎫
for yᵉ Clery Storyes, ₴ mendyng of xxxvᵘ olde⎪ **xvijd.**
barres, vijd.; ₴ for yᵉ mendyng of yᵉ laten⎪
Censors ⁽³⁸⁾ at Norwyche, vd. . . . . ⎭

Itm̃ payed to John Wodcocke for pte of yᵉ fferme of⎫ **iijs. vjd.**
sᵖrten londs lyeng wᵗin yᵉ ffolde Course of Elmhm̃⎭

ᴸtsicquieti  Sum̃, xxvjs. ixd.
ñt dicti
Villm̃ᵍ et  The sum̃e of yᵉ Reč of yᵉ seyd Wyllm̃ ₴ Ed-⎫
ᴸdmñdᵍ  mñde ys . . . . . . ⎬ iiijli. xiiijs. ijd., ₴ xvjd.
ᵣo hoc Aᵒ  The sum̃e of yᵉ Expenss ₴ Charges of yᵉ seyd⎫
ᵖdicto.  Wyllm̃ ffranckelyng And Edmñde ffletcher . ⎬ iiijli. xjs. vijd.

E

And so remayn in yᵉʳ hands As ys here layed down $\Big\}$ ijs. viijd.
by them at yᵉʳ Accomptes in monye  .   .   .
And so the seyd Wyllm̃ ffranckelyng ɀ Edmñde ffletcher be clerly
dyscharged for thys yere paste.


A° Dom.                              A° dm. 1546°.
1546.
[A° 38°   Mᵈ. A Rekenyng made yᵉ Wedñsedaye in Whyghtsonweke, the
Hen.VIII.]    yere of owʳ lorde M¹¹ccccc ɀ xlvjᵗⁱ, of Edmñde ffletcher ɀ Thoñs
              powle for Wyllm̃ dycke, because he refused shortlye aft̃ he was
              chosen, ɀc., Chyrchewardens of Northelmhm̃.
              In p̃imis Receyuid at yᵉ Accompts As ys Afore $\Big\}$ ijs. viijd.
              specified  .   .   .   .   .   .   .   .   .
              Itm̃ reč of Alyˢ m̃ᵒchall of Bylney, wydow, ɀ Jo͠hn hyr $\Big\}$ xiijs. iiijd.
              sone for lond ferme lyeng wᵗin betele  .   .   .
furres        Itm̃ reč of Herry Greye of Bresele for furres  .   .        iiijd.
soulde.       Itm̃ reč of Thoñs Lussher for yᵉ ferme of yᵉ Campyng $\Big\}$ iiijs.
              Closse ɀ other londs  .   .   .   .   .   .
              Itm̃ reč of Jaffrye Rudd for londe ferme  .   .   .          xd.
              Itm̃ reč of Roberd Rudd of Betele for londe ferme yᵉʳ   ixs.  vjd.
              Itm̃ reč of Wyllm̃ yarrhm̃ for yᵉ ferme of yᵉ Town $\Big\}$ xxijs.
              Closse ɀ other londs  .   .   .   .   .   .
              Itm̃ reč of Thoñs Shetell for londe ferme  .   .   .  iiijs.  xd.
              Itm̃ reč of Herry Ruston for londe ferme  .   .   .        ijs.
              Itm̃ reč of Nycholas purdy for londe ferme.               xvjd.
              Itm̃ reč of Wyllm̃ ffranckelyng for londe ferme  .   .     xijd.
              Itm̃ reč of John Hall of Bctele for londe ferme  .   .     ijs.
              Itm̃ reč of Añe Taůner of Bresesele (sic) ⁽³⁹⁾, for $\Big\}$ vs.
              londe ferme lyeng wᵗiu her grett Closse in yᵉ
              pasture yˡˢ yere ɀ other beying paste  .

Itm̃ reč of Nycholas dyght for londe ferme in yᵉ
pasture heyred of John Wodcoke by the wholl
townchype yᵉʳ as longe as he hys *(sic)* fermour of
them . . . . . . . . . } vijs.

Itm̃ reč of Edmñde ffletcher for londe ferme ther
heyred of yᵉ seyd John Wodcoke by the seyd
townchype in mañ aforseyd . . . . . } iiijs.

Itm̃ reč of Wyllm̃ Euᵖode of Gatele for londe ferme yᵉʳ
heyred of yᵉ seyed John Wodcoke by the seyd
townchype in mañ aforseyd . . . . } vs.

Mᵈ. ther remayned yˡᵉ yere nothyng of yᵉ pfyghts of Halowmes
nyght, all thyngs dyscharged due to be payed yᵉⁿ, s. for yᵉ
wasshyng of yᵉ Syrpleses, tendyng of yᵉ bells, ℥ suche other.
And to John Wryght for mendyng of Certen yron worcke
longyng to yᵉ Chyrche, but ijs. iiijᵈ., wyche monye Thom̃s powle
Aforseyd reč for iiij bʒ of Malte, to be delyuᵖyd Ageynst the
next Halowmes by hyᵖ or his Assynes, wᵗ A hepe at ye Combʒ.

Itm̃ reč by me, yᵉ seyd Edmñde ffletcher, of sᵖ John
Eluᵖyche, iijs. iiijᵈ., in pte of xvijs. iiijᵈ. which he
had in his Custodye, belongyng to yᵉ Chyrche gate
plow ther ⁽⁴⁰⁾, ℥ yᵉ rest, whyche was xiiijs., was
delyuᵖed to Wyllm̃ Thompson ℥ Nycholas purdy,
Constables ther, by the seyd sᵖ John Eluᵖyche, ℥
by the consent of yᵉ Inhabitance ther, for necessary
chargs belongyng to yᵉ town, ℥ so He ys dyscharged
of yᵉ wholl . . . . . . . . } iijs. iiijᵈ.

Sum̃ tota p͟ᶜᵉdens reč, iiijˡⁱ. viijs. viijᵈ.

These be y<sup>e</sup> Charges & Expensis leyd owte & payed by the seyd Edmñde ffletcher & Thoñs powle the yere of ower Lorde god Aforseyd, &c.

| | |
|---|---:|
| In p⁰imis for lyght & offeryng at y<sup>e</sup> obyte day for the benefactours vpon Wyghtson wedñsdaye y<sup>e</sup> laste yere . . . . . . . . . | ij*d*. |
| Itñ for lyght & offering at y<sup>e</sup> obyte day of M⁹ Smythe & Collett his wyffe, Alwayes kept vpon Holy Rode daye (41) . . . . . . . . . | ij*d*. |
| Itñ to Margaret Croker for mēdyng of A Syrples . | j*d*. oƀ |
| Itñ to John Gogney for y<sup>e</sup> Rent of y<sup>e</sup> town londs of Elmhñ lyeng w<sup>t</sup>in y<sup>e</sup> fylds of Betele . . . | v*s*. |
| Itñ to Rychard Ruston & John Pers, Constables ther, to be payed towards y<sup>e</sup> kepyng of y<sup>e</sup> bekon watche | ij*s*. |
| Itñ to Margaret Croker for y<sup>e</sup> mēdyng of a Ratchet . | j*d*. |
| Itñ payed to y<sup>e</sup> lords Collectour for y<sup>e</sup> m̃cyment of A weye lyeng at wodforthe . . . . . | xij*d*. |
| Itñ to John Brown, being y<sup>e</sup> seyd lords Collectour y<sup>er</sup>, for y<sup>e</sup> lete fee of y<sup>e</sup> town londs of Northelmhñ lyeng in Betele . . . . . . . | xxiiij*s*. |
| redd sol⁰. Itñ to y<sup>e</sup> seyd John Brown for y<sup>e</sup> rent of the town londs of Northelmhñ Aforseyd . . . . | vij*s*. |
| Itñ to Wyllñ yarrhñ for y<sup>e</sup> makyng of y<sup>e</sup> gret bell whele . . . . . . . . . | iij*s*. iiij*d*. |
| Itñ for A gret lantorn to bear lyght before y<sup>e</sup> Sacramēt (42) . . . . . . . . | vj*d*. |
| Itñ to Thoñs Shetell for y<sup>e</sup> Carryeng of ij lodes of Grauell to Woodforthe . . . . . . | viij*d*. |

Suñ, xliiij*s*. oƀ.

Itm̃ payed to Wyllm̃ Thomson ҁ Nycholas purdy,
Co͝stables yᵉʳ, to be payed towards yᵉ kypyng of ⎱ ijs.
bekon watche, ҁc.   .   .   .   .   .   .

Itm̃ to my lady hastyngs balye for Rent of s͝rten londs ⎱ vjd.
longyng to yᵉ town of Elmhm̃ ҁ holden of her   .

Itm̃ to one James, A Taylour of ffolsehm̃, for yᵉ ⎱ xijd.
mendyng of yᵉ Redd Cope ⁽⁴³⁾ rownde Abowte

Itm̃ payed to yᵉ Constables of Betele for the taxe of yᵉ ⎱ vs.
town londs of Northelmhm̃ yᵉʳ   .   .   .   .

Itm̃ to John Wryght for makyng of yᵉ Chyrche dore
keye ҁ for yᵉ mendyng also of the locke ҁ keye ⎰ viijd.
of yᵉ Chest yᵗ standythe in yᵉ quere by the
Sepulcre ⁽⁴⁴⁾ .   .   .   .   .   .   .   .

Itm̃ to yᵉ Constables of Gressenhall for yᵉ taxe of ⎱ ijd.
s͝rten londs .   .   .   .   .   .   .   .

Itm̃ to John Wryght for yᵉ mc̄dyng of yᵉ iijᵗʰ bell ⎱ ijs.   ijd.
clapper .   .   .   .   .   .   .   .   .

Itm̃ payed to John Wodcoke for serten londs lyeng wᵗin
yᶜ pasture ҁ heyred of hym frō tyme to tyme by
the Chyrchwardens yᵉʳ, xixs. vjd., ҁ hathe bownde
hym selfe by pmyse to yᵉ townchype yᵉʳ yᵗ they
shall have yᵉᵐ so long As he ys ffermoʳ, ҁ no other
to have yᵉᵐ but yᵉⁱ (sic), so he be payed euⁿy yere ⎰ xixs.   vjd.
afore hande ye sume Aforseyd in man͠ ҁ fourme
As ys Agreed betwyxe yᵉ Inhabitan͠ce of ye
townchype of Elmhm̃ ҁ hym, whereof pte ys
payed of yᵉ receyts for yᵉ ferme of yᵉ seyd londs
and yᵉ rest of yᵉʳ other pfyghts belongyng to yᵉ
town, wyche ys comōly iijs. vjd. at yᵉ leste wayes .

Itm̃ for yᵉ mendyng yᵉ waye at byllyngforde brydge ⎰ xiiijd.

E 2

This entry is crossed out. Itm̃ payed to Roger Hamonde for yᵉ fellyng of A troe to mende wᵗ yᵉ brydge by father Rudds . . } iij𝑑.

Itm̃ in Expenss at Estderhm̃ for my ptener ꝫ me whan we were Comãded to Apere before yᶜ Com̃yssyoners yᵉʳ ꝫ to bryng A true Certyficat of all suche Chantryes and ppetuytyes ⁽⁴⁵⁾ As wer wᵗin yᵉ town yᵉʳ, ꝫc. . . . . . . } viij𝑑.

Itm̃ payed to Mʳᵉˢ dethyke for yᵉ mendyng of yᵉ best Canapye ⁽⁴⁶⁾, yᵉ Crosse clothe of sylk ⁽⁴⁷⁾, ꝫ yᵉ Cope ⁽⁴⁸⁾ that ys grene and full of Roses, ꝫc. . } iiij𝑑.

Itm̃ payed to sᵍ John Eluᵖyche for yᵉ wryghtyng of owʳ sᵖtyfycat Aforseyd, wyche was payed by hyᵖ to yᵉ Clerks of yᵉ seyd com̃yssyoners . . . . } ij𝑑.

Sum̃, xxxiijs. iiij𝑑.

The sum̃e of yᵉ Receyts of yᵉ seyd Edmñde ꝫ Thom̃s ys . . . . . . . . } iiij𝑙𝑖. viijs. viij𝑑.

The sum̃e of the Expenss ꝫ Charges of yᵉ seyd Edmñde ffletcher ꝫ Thom̃s powle . } ys iij𝑙𝑖. xvijs. iij𝑑. oᵬ

And so remayn in yᵉʳ hands in monye As ys here leyd down at ther Accomptes, ꝫc. . . . . } xjs. iiij𝑑. oᵬ*

And so the seyd Edmñde ffletcher ꝫ Thom̃s powle be clerly dyscharged for yᵉ yere that ys paste.

Aᵒ Dm. 1547. [Aᵒ 1ᵒ Edw. VI.]

Anno dm̃ 1547.

Mᵈ. A Rekenyng made yᵉ Wedñsdaye in Whyghtsone Weke the yere of owʳ lorde god Mᵘ ccccc ꝫ xlvijᵗ¹ of Thom̃s powle And Rychard Ruston, Chyrchwardens of Northelmhm̃.

In pᵖimis Reĉ at yᵉ Accompts of yᵉ seyd xjs. iij𝑑. (? iiij𝑑.) oᵬ afore specyfyed* . . . . . } xs.

Itm̃ reč for yᵉ pfyght of Halowmes nyght wᵗ yᵉ viijd. \
that ffather Rudd gafe to yᵉ Chyrche vjs. vjd. \
whereof payed yᵉⁿ for yᵉ wasshȳg of yᵉ Chyrche \
gere xvjd.; to Rychard Rust for iiij bȝ of malte yᵉ } iijs.  ixd. \
next yere wᵗ A hepe at yᵉ Combe ijs. ijd.; ȝ so \
remayn in yᵉʳ hande iijs. ixd. . . . . /

Itm̃ Reč of Thom̃s Lussher for yᵉ fferme of yᵉ Cãpyng- }
closse . . . . . . . . . } ijs.

Itm̃ reč of hym for other londs wᵗin Elmhm̃ ffylds . ijs.

Itm̃ reč of Elyn Rudd, wydow, for londe fferme yᵉʳ . xd.

Itm̃ reč of Nycholas purdy for londe fferme yᵉʳ . . xvjd.

Itm̃ reč of Herry Rustñ for londe fferme yᵉʳ . . ijs.

Suñ, xxjs. xjd.

Elmhm̃.

Itm̃ reč of Wyllm̃ yarrhm̃ for londe fferme yᵉʳ . ijs.

Itm̃ reč of Shetell Thom̃s for londe fferme yᵉʳ . iiijs. xd.

Itm̃ reč of John Johnson for londe fferme yᵉʳ . xijd.

Itm̃ reč of Wyllm̃ ffranckelyng for londe fferme yᵉʳ xijd.

Betele.

Itm̃ reč of yᵉ wydow of Bylney yᵗ kepe yᵉ psons howse \
ȝ hyr sone s. of Alys Marche ȝ John hyr sone for \
yᵉ fferme of xxᵗⁱ Acrᵖ of londs lyeng wᵗin yᵉ } xiijs. iiijd. \
Town ȝ ffylds of Betelee . . . . .

Itm̃ reč of Robt Rudd for viij Acrᵖ yᵉʳ ynclosed . . viijs.

Itm̃ reč of hym for iij Acrᵖ yᵉʳ lyeng in his Closse . ijs.

Itm̃ reč of John Halle for ij Acrᵖ lyeng yᵉʳ . . ijs. iiijd.

Itm̃ reč of Wyllm̃ yarrhm̃ for A Closse lyeng yᵉʳ . xxs.

Itm̃ reč for Crocks ȝ Trenchers⁽⁴⁹⁾ solde at Mychael- }
mes by the Chyrchewardens then, ȝc . . . } xiiijd.

Itm̃ reč of Nycholas dyght for londe fferme lyeng in y$^e$
pasture & heyred of John Woodcoke by y$^e$ vij$s$.
Chyrchewardens . . . . . . .

Itm̃ reč of Edmñde ffletcher for londe fferme y$^{er}$ heyred
of y$^e$ seyd John Woodcoke by the seyd Chyrche- iiij$s$.
wardens . . . . . . .

Itm̃ reč of Wyllm̃ Eu$^9$ode, of Gatele, for londe fferme
y$^{er}$ heyred of y$^e$ seyd John Woodcocke, by the v$s$.
seyd Chyrchwardens . . . . .

Sum̃, iij$li$. xj$s$. vij$d$.

These be y$^e$ Chargs & Expenss leyed owte & payed by the seyd
Thom̃s Powle & Rychard Rustñ the yere of ow$^r$ Lord god
aforseyd, &c.

In p$^9$imis for lyght & offeryng at y$^e$ obyte daye of all
y$^e$ benefactours now depted, & other . . . ij$d$.

Itm̃ payed to Rychard Goose for A Swerde for A
Sowdyour, &c. . . . . . . xx$d$.

Itm̃ leyed owte for whytlether for y$^e$ baderycks . . iiij$d$.

Itm̃ to a plūmer for y$^e$ remouyng & sowdyng of y$^e$ ledd
& mendyng of y$^e$ Tymbre worcke also vpon y$^e$ xij$d$.
nether pte of the pynnacle of y$^e$ Steple, ij dayes .

Itm̃ for v$^{li}$ & di. of sowde for y$^e$ seyd worcke . ij$s$. iiij$d$.

Itm̃ for hys Comons the seyd ij dayes . . . vj$d$.

Itm̃ for hys s$^9$uers wags & Comõs y$^e$ seyd ij dayes . viij$d$.

Itm̃ for nayle y$^{en}$, iiij$d$.; for wodd y$^{en}$ for y$^e$ plūmer, ij$d$. vj$d$.

Sum̃, vij$s$. ij$d$.

Itm̃ to Wyllm̃ ffyncke for layeng of y$^e$ breke in y$^e$ ij
panes of y$^e$ wyndow vpon y$^e$ bellsoller ij dayes &
di., for his Comons y$^e$ seyd tyme, & for sowde also ij$s$. ij$d$.
to tempre w$^t$ y$^e$ ledd, &c. . . . .

| | | | |
|---|---|---|---|
| | Itm̃ for his s'uers wags & Comons y^e seyd tyme . . | | viijd. |
| | Itm̃ to Rychard ffranckelyng for lyme & breke for y^e panes of y^e seyd wyndow, &c. . . . . . | | xijd. |
| | Itm̃ for woode, ijd.; & to Wyllm̃ yarrhm̃ for y^e wyndow y^t hangeth in y^e mydle pane of the wyndow vpon y^e belsoller, xijd. . . . . . . . . . | | xiiijd. |
| | Itm̃ payed to my lady Hastyngs (50) baly for Rent . | | vjd. |
| | Itm̃ payed to Wryght for a bolte for y^e grett bell, xijd.; for yrons for y^e seyd bell, iiijd.; & for A dagger for A Sowdyour, viijd. . . . . . . . | ijs. | |
| | Itm̃ to Reyner for Tendyng of y^e bells, vjd. And to Willm̃ yarrhm̃ also for y^e trym̃yng of y^em, xvjd. . | | xxijd. |
| | Sum̃, ixs. iiijd. | | |
| | Itm̃ payed to Rob̃t Barchrhm̃ for y^e sawyng of y^e Tree wherew^t was made y^e brydge by Rudds. . . | vijs. | viijd. |
| | Itm̃ for y^e makyng of A pytt to saw y^e seyd tree, iiijd.; & vnto John̄ Lamberd for ij bytts of y^e same tree, viijd. . . . . . . . . . . . | | xijd. |
| | Itm̃ payed for A Syrples & y^e makyng thereof . . | vjs. | viijd. |
| | Itm̃ payed to good Beales of Byllyngford for y^e Caryage of ij Tables for Aulters (51) frō Norwyche | | xijd. |
| Redd sol' | Itm̃ payed to y^e Lords Colour for the Rent of the Town londs of Northelmhm̃, &c. . . . . . . | vijs. | |
| | Itm̃ for makyng of y^e Chyldren Coopes, xvjd.; to y^e Ryngers whan we kept for o^r late sou'ayn Lorde kyng Henry the viij^th (52), iiijd.; & for offeryng, jd. | | xxjd. |
| | Sum̃, xxvs. jd. | | |
| | Itm̃ payed to y^e Lords Colour for y^e lete ffee of y^e Town londs of Elmhm̃ lyeng y^er & yn Bettele, &c. | xxiiijs. | |

Itm̃ payed to yᵉ seyd Colour for yᵉ Rent of yᵉ Town londs of Elmhm̃ lyeng wᵗin Betele . . . } vs.

Itm̃ payed to John Wryght for hengles, hokes, ₲ A barre for yᵉ wyndow vpon bellsoller . . . } iiijd.

✠ solde by Rychard Ruston ₲ John Pers, Chyrchwardens yᵉⁿ, by the Consente and Assent of dyu⁹se of yᵉ Inhabytance yᵉʳ yᵉ iiijᵗʰ daye of Jñe, A° dm̃ 1547°, ₲ A° 1° Ed. Sixti, fyrste for A Monstrant of Sylu⁹ ⁽⁵³⁾ pcell gylte, xxjᵗˡ vncs j qter ₲ d. aft̃ iiijs. vjd. yᵉ vnce, iiijli. xvjs. A payer of Sensors wᵗ yᵉ shype of Sylu⁹ ⁽⁵⁴⁾, xxxijᵗˡ vncs aft̃ iiijs. vjd. yᵉ vnce, vijli. iiijs. A payer of paxes of Sylu⁹ ⁽⁵⁵⁾ pcell gylte, xjᵗʰ vncs, d. ljs. ixd. The wholle Sum̃ xiiijli. xjs. ixd., yᵉ reste was rec̃ yn the exchange of A payer of Chalyce ⁽⁵⁶⁾, ₲c., ut seq̃ ibm̃.

Itm̃ payed to John Woodcoke for Certen londs lyeng wᵗin yᵉ pasture beyonde yᵉ Hey Crosse to Ryborough warde ⁽⁵⁷⁾ ₲ heyred by the Chyrche- } xixs. vjd. wardens of Northelmhm̃ to ₲ for yᵉ entents ₲ purposes Afore exp⁹ssed, ₲c. . . . . .

Sum̃, xlviijs. xd.

The sum̃e of yᵉ Receyts of yᵉ seyd Thom̃s ₲ Rychard ys . . . . . . . } iiijli. xiijs. vijd.

The sum̃e of ther Expenss ₲ Charges thys yere ys . iiijli. xs. vd.

And so remayn in ther hands As here ys leyd down At yᵉʳ Accompts besyds all thyngs aforseyd dys- } iijs. ijd. charged . . . . . . . . .

And so the. seyd Thom̃s Powle ₲ Rychard Rustñ And yᵉʳ Heyres be clerly dyscharged for yˡˢ } et sic q⁹eti sñt, yere paste . . . . . . . . ₲c.

A° Dm.  A° dm. 1548°.

1548.
[A° 2°
lw. VI.]
M<sup>d</sup>. A Rekenyng made y<sup>e</sup> Wedñsedaye in Wyghtsone weke, the yere of ow<sup>r</sup> Lord god M<sup>ll</sup>ccccc ҩ xlviij<sup>th</sup> of Rychard Rustñ ҩ John Pers, Chyrchewardens of northelmhm̃ the same yere, ҩc.

In p<sup>9</sup>imis reč At y<sup>e</sup> Accompts As ys afore specyfyed . iijs. ijd.

Itm̃ reč then of Rychard C<sup>r</sup>owe for A Medow lyeng w<sup>t</sup>in Byttryng, one yere . . . . ijs. viijd.

Itm̃ reč y<sup>en</sup> of Thom̃s Shetell for A tre Toppe . . xijd.

Itm̃ reč y<sup>en</sup> for wodd solde in y<sup>e</sup> Town Closse in Betele to s<sup>9</sup>ten dyu<sup>9</sup>se of Elmhm̃ . . . . . ijs. iiijd.

The wholl reč at y<sup>e</sup> seyd Accompts . . . . ixs. ijd.

Itm̃ reč of Herry Grenwode for s<sup>9</sup>rten plat ✚ set owt in fine, hoc signo, ҩc., ibm̃ . . . xvjli. xvjs. iiijd.

Itm̃ reč for y<sup>e</sup> Clothes y<sup>t</sup> henge before y<sup>e</sup> roode lofte w<sup>t</sup> other small steyned clothes ҩ y<sup>e</sup> ymages <sup>(58)</sup> . ixs. ijd.

Sum̃, xvijli. vs. vjd., besyds y<sup>e</sup> seyd ixs. ijd.

Itm̃ reč of s<sup>9</sup>rten w<sup>t</sup>in Elmham̃, Bettele, ҩ Bylneye, for lond ferme, s. of Alys Marche ҩ John her sone, xiijs. iiijd.; of Robt Rudd, xs.; of Wyllm̃ Sohm̃, ijs. iiijd.; of Herry Rustñ, iiijd.; of Thom̃s Lussher, vs. iiijd.; of Nycholas Purdy, xvjd.; of Henry Rustñ, ijs.; of Cateryng dyght, vijs.; of Edmñde ffletcher, iiijs.; of Wyllm̃ Eu<sup>9</sup>ode, vs. . ls. viijd.

Sum̃, ls. viijd.

Itm̃ reč of Wyllm̃ ffra<sup>9</sup>ckelynge for lond ferme, xijd.; of John Brown for londe ferme, xvd.; of Thom̃s Shetell for lond fferme, iiijs. xd.; of John Johnson for londe ferme, xijd. . . . . . viijs. jd.

Sum̃, viijs. jd.

Expenss ҩ Charges leyd owte by the seyd Chyrche Wardens the yere aforseyd, ҩc.

|  |  |  |
|---|---|---|
| In pᵒimis for yᵉ lyght and offeryng for yᵉ bᵒnfactors . |  | ijd. |
| Itm̄ for lether for yᵉ baderycks, viijd.; ҩ to Wyllm̄ Tylney for hys fee of reparyng yᵉ wyndowes, xijd. |  | xxd. |
| Itm̄ for yᵉ Taxe of yᵉ Town Londs in Betele . . | vs. | ijd. |
| Itm̄ for yᵉ Taxe of yᵉ Town Londs in Elmhm̄ . . | vs. | viijd. |
| Itm̄ payed to Mᵒ Robt Curson for sᵒrten Rearages for Londs longyng to yᵉ Chapell of Becke,⁽⁵⁹⁾ ҩc. . | | xxiiijs. |
| Itm̄ to yᵉ Colour for yᵒ lete fee of yᵉ man̄ of Elmhm̄ | | xxiiijs. |
| Itm̄ for yᵉ Chargs of Margaret Nycholls ҩ her kepers the tymo of her syknes the yere that ys paste . | | ijs. |

Redd solᵖ Itm̄ for yᵉ Rent of yᵉ Town londs of Elmhm̄, vijs., ҩ Betele, vs. . . . . . . . . } xijs.

Nᵒ hic ᵖ Itm̄ payed for A Byble, xvs., ҩ yᵉ paraphrasys of Erasmo ⁽⁶⁰⁾ vpon yᵉ Gospells ҩ yᵉ Actes of yᵉ Apostles, xijs., ҩc.. . . . . . . } xxvijs.

Itm̄ to ffyncke for glasyng, ijs.; for lyme, ijs.; for yᵉ caryage of yᵉ seyd lyme, xvjd. To Woodcoke for londe fermo be syds the receyts for his londe, iijs. vjd. . . . . . . . . } viijs. xd.

Sum̄, vli. xs. vjd.

|  |  |
|---|---|
| Itm̄ payed for yᵉ wasshyng of yᵉ Chyrche gere . . | xvjd. |
| Itm̄ putt ynto yᵉ poore folcks Cheste at yᵉ quere doro⁽⁶¹⁾ | iijs. iiijd. |
| Itm̄ in Chargs at Walsynghm̄ ⁽⁶²⁾ before yᵉ kyngs vysytours ҩ Com̄yssyoncrs for owʳ expenss ҩ bylls wryttē by yᵉᵐ ҩ leyd owt by vs yᵉʳ . . . | xxd. |
| Itm̄ to Wyllm̄ Tylney for yᵉ Colouryng of yᵉ panes of yᵉ Table at yᵉ Hygh Aulter ⁽⁶³⁾ ҩ yᵉ fore pt of yᵉ rode lofte . . . . . . . | iijs. iiijd. |

N⁰.  Itm̃ to yᵉ baly of yᵉ hūdered towards yˢ makyng of yᵉ ⎫
       bekons . . . . . . . . . ⎭  xxd.

Itm̃ to John Wryght for yᵉ mēdyng of y⁰ locke vpon ⎫
  yᵉ Steple dore ⅋ A new key therto, vijd.; for ⎪
  Mendyng yᵉ locke ⅋ A new key for yᵉ pore folcks ⎪
  Cheste, vjd.; ⅋ for ij hengells for yᵉ gates at yᵉ ⎬  xvijd.
  Hethe, ijd.; for mēdyng A bolte of yᵉ gret bell ⅋ ⎪
  other small yrons to yᵉ same, ijd. . . . . ⎭

Itm̃ for d. A bꝛ of Whete for bred Ageynst Halowmes      iiijd.
Itm̃ for ij locks to hange vpon yᵉ pore folcks Cheste .      viijd.
Itm̃ to Herry Wells for yᵉ tendyng of yᵉ bells . .      vjd.
Itm̃ to Watson ⅋ Thompsō for makyng yᵉ dytche at ⎫
  fulfurth dale betwen Gatle ⅋ vs . . . . ⎭  xviijd.

Itm̃ to John Wryght for Mendyng ⅋ lenghyng y⁰ ⎫
  barres of yᵉ southe grat ⅋ yrons for yᵉ fall Gat at ⎬  xviijd.
  Geloms . . . . . . . . . ⎭

Itm̃ to Herry my sone for hys worckemāshype of yᵉ ⎫
  seyd grat, xviijd., ⅋ to ffather Here helpyng hym ⎬  xxijd.
  ther, iiijd. . . . . . . . . ⎭

Sum̃, xixs. jd.


Itm̃ to yᵉ becon watche, ijs.  To Thom̃s powle for to ⎫
  bye bowes ⅋ Arowes, xs., ⅋ for A Casse for A ⎪
  Shefe of Arowes, xijd.  To Wyllm̃ fyncke in pt ⎬ xxiijs.
  of paymēt of xxs. for yᵉ whytyng of yᵉ Chyrche, ⎪
  xs. . . . . . . . . . ⎭

Itm̃ for yᵉ makyng of yᵉ Comon butts, yᵉ grauyng of yᵉ ⎫
  flaggs, ⅋ makyng yᵉ dytches Abowte yᵉ seyd butts ⎭  vs. viijd.

Itm̃ for yᵉ Caryeng of x lods of flaggs for yᵉ seyd butts ⎫
  wᵗ myn own Carte, aft iijd. yᵉ lode . . ⎭  ijs. vjd.

Itm̃ payed to Mother dunkhm̃ for A Tubb for the⎫  
Chyrche whygthyng, iiijd.; for A matte for y<sup>em</sup> ⎪  
y<sup>t</sup> reade vpon y<sup>e</sup> byble ȝ y<sup>e</sup> paraphrass, jd.; for ⎪  
wodde, jd.; for y<sup>e</sup> helpyng vp of y<sup>e</sup> large ladders ⎬    viijd.  
in y<sup>e</sup> Chyrche vpon y<sup>e</sup> worckyng dayes, in drynoke, ⎪  
ijd.   .   .   .   .   .   .   .   . ⎭

Itm̃ in Expenss at Walsynghm̃ for ow<sup>r</sup> horsemete not ⎫    iiijd.  
wrytte<sup>9</sup> Amongst ow<sup>r</sup> chargs y<sup>er</sup> Aforseyd   .   . ⎭

Som̃e, xxxijs. ijd., ȝc.

☞     Thes Sum̃es folowyng wer leyd owte by John pers—  
Itm̃ payed for v daggers for y<sup>e</sup> Sowdyours ther   .   .    iij<i>s</i>. iiij<i>d</i>.  

Itm̃ for A Scaberd for A Swerd ȝ Another for A ⎫  
daggerd   .   .   .   .   .   .   . ⎭    viij<i>d</i>.  

Itm̃ for y<sup>e</sup> Caryeng of vij lods of fflaggs to Como<sup>9</sup> butts    xxj<i>d</i>.  

Itm̃ for v newe Swerds for y<sup>e</sup> Sowdyours ther the p̃yce ⎫  
of eu<sup>9</sup>y one of them, ij<i>s</i>. viij<i>d</i>.   .   .   . ⎬ xiij<i>s</i>. iiij<i>d</i>.  

Itm̃ in Expenss for my selffe ȝ my horse whan I bowt ⎫  
y<sup>e</sup> seyd Swerds ȝ daggers; for I Rod fyrste to ⎬    v<i>d</i>.  
Alsehm̃ ffayer, ȝ from thēse to Norwyche   . ⎭

Som̃e xix<i>s</i>. vj<i>d</i>. besyds the Som̃e yerly payed to John ⎫  
Wodcoke for londs heyred of hym by the Tow<sup>9</sup>- ⎬ xix<i>s</i>.   vj<i>d</i>.  
chype, ȝ lyeng in y<sup>e</sup> pasture, wyche ys.   .   . ⎭

Itm̃ for Mendyng of y<sup>e</sup> fall gat at y<sup>e</sup> olde pale, ȝ for ⎫  
Wood for y<sup>e</sup> mēdyng of y<sup>e</sup> hedge y<sup>er</sup>, ȝ for y<sup>e</sup> ⎬    viij<i>d</i>.  
caryēg of y<sup>e</sup> same   .   .   .   .   . ⎭

☞ The wholl Sum̃ to be rekened frō y<sup>is</sup> sygne Aforseyd ys, xl<i>s</i>. ij<i>d</i>.

The Sume of y⁰ Rcc̃ of y⁰ seyd Rychard ℈ John ys xx*li*. xiij*s*. v*d*.

The Suṁe of y⁰ʳ Exponss this yere ys . . . x*li*. xxiij*d*.

And so remayn in ther hands As ys her leyd down ⎫
at y⁰ʳ Accompts besyds all thyngs dyscharged ⎬ x*li*. vj*s*. (?) vj*d*.
due to be rekned thē . . . . . ⎭

And so y⁰ seyd Rychard Rustñ ℈ John Pers ℈ y⁰ʳ heyres be clerlye dyscharged for this yere that ys paste.

Mᵈ yᵗ ther remayned of y⁰ Rec̃ aforseyd, wyche are in y⁰ wholl Soṁe xx*li*. xiij*s*. v*d*. taken owt therof for y⁰ Chargs aforseyd, x*li*. vj*s*. vj*d*., ℈ so remayned xj*li*. ix*s*. vj*d*., wᵗ the rest receyyed then for sᵖrten thyngs sold at yᵗ tyme wherof was payed than to Wyllm̃ ffyncke in full cōtentacon ℈ paymēt of xx*s*. for y⁰ whyghtyng of y⁰ Chyrche, x*s*., ℈ ij*s*. yᵗ they gaue hym. Aud pte of y⁰ Rest of y⁰ seyd xj*li*. ix*s*. vj*d*. wyche was iiij*s*. vj*d*. was payed thē to sᵖrten of y⁰ Townchype wyche had payed yᵗ afore to y⁰ bekon watche, ℈ so remayn clere in y⁰ hands of y⁰ new Chyrche wardens but x*li*. xiij*s*. As ys aforseyd, wherof remayn in y⁰ hands of John pers the olde Chyrche warden, v*li*., ℈ y⁰ rest wyche ys v*li*. xiij*s*. remayn in y⁰ hands of Wyllm̃ ffranckelyng, whom he hath chosen to be hys felowe for yˡˢ ycre comyng, ℈c.

Mᵈ. aff⁹ ye Rekenyng made the seyd John Pers hathe ⎫
Chosñ Wyllm̃ ffranckelyng to be hys felow for⎮
thys yere Comyng As ys aforseyd ℈ delyu⁹ed y⁰ᵐ ⎮
in hande As ys Afore wrytten on y⁰ other syde, ⎬x*li*. xiij*s*.
x*li*. xiij*s*. wherof remayn in y⁰ hands of John⎮
Pers, v*li*., ℈ in y⁰ hands of Wyllm̃ ffranckelyng,⎮
v*li*. xiij*s*. as ys also Afore wrytten, ℈c. . . . ⎭

A° Dm.                              Anno dm̄ 1549°.

1549.     M<sup>d</sup>. A Rekenyng made vpon Trynytie Sondaye aft̆ Euyngsong the
[A° 3°     yere of o<sup>r</sup> Lord god м<sup>ll</sup>cccc ҩ xlix<sup>th</sup> of John Pers And Wyllm̄
Edw. VI.] ffranckelyng, Chyrchewardens of northelmhm̄ the same yere.

Receyts by  In p<sup>9</sup>imis Reč at y<sup>e</sup> Accompts as ys aforseyd  .  . v*li*. xiijs.
Wyt̄ffra<sup>9</sup>ck  Itm̄ reč of Richard peers gyffne by the same Rychard ⎫
            towards y<sup>e</sup> mendyng of y<sup>•</sup> noysome wayes w<sup>t</sup>in ⎬ iij*li*. vjs. viijd.
            y<sup>e</sup> Town ҩ Stretes of northelmhm̄  .  .  . ⎭

            Itm̄ reč of M<sup>res</sup> dethyk, xiijs. iiijd. beyng pcell of her ⎫
            husbonds quethode to the seyd Entens .      . ⎬ xiijs. iiijd.

            Itm̄ reč of Rychard Crow for lond fferme         . ijs. viijd.
Lo<sup>9</sup> ff. in Bet  Itm̄ reč for An olde Aulter cloth .    .    .    .        iijd.

                                        Sum̄, ix*li*. xvs. xjd.

Bet.       Itm̄ reč of John m<sup>9</sup>che for lond ferme in Betele .  . xiijs. iiijd.
Bet.       Itm̄ reč of Roberd Rudd for lond ferme y<sup>er</sup> .  .  . xs.
Lo<sup>9</sup> ff. w<sup>t</sup>in  Itm̄ reč of Rychard Crow for lond ferme, ijs. viijd.; of
Betele ҩ     Thom̄s Lussher for y<sup>e</sup> Campyng Closse, iijs. iiijd., ⎫
Elmhm̄.       ҩ for londs in the ffylds, ijs.; of Thom̄s Shetell for ⎪
             lond fferme, iiijs. xd.; of John Johnson for lond ⎬ xxxs.  xd.
             fferme, xijd.; ҩ of Wyllm̄ yarrhm̄ for o<sup>r</sup> Closse at ⎪
             Betele, xxs. And for lond fferme lyeng w<sup>t</sup>in ⎪
             Elmhm̄, ijs. .  .   .    .    .    .    .    . ⎭

            Itm̄ reč of Rob̄t Twayts s. for y<sup>e</sup> pte of Chryste ⎫
            Chyrche <sup>(64)</sup> for y<sup>•</sup> halfe p<sup>9</sup>yce of y<sup>e</sup> Byble ҩ y<sup>•</sup> ⎬ xiijs.
            paraphrass .    .    .    .    .    .    . ⎭

                                        Sum̄, iij*li*. xijs. ijd.

Lo<sup>9</sup>ff. in bet  Itm̄ reč of Wyllm̄ Sohm̄ for londe fferme  .    . ijs. viijd.
ҩ Elmhm̄.   Itm̄ reč of John Brown meas<sup>9</sup> for lond fferme  .  . xvd.
            Itm̄ reč for y<sup>e</sup> Com̄o waxe y<sup>t</sup> was solde   .   . xxijs.
            Itm̄ reč of Wyllm̄ Eu<sup>9</sup>ode for londe fferme in Elmhm̄ . vs.
                                        Sum̄, xxxs. xjd.

The Wholl Sum̃ Aforseyd rec̃ by the seyd Wyllm̃ ffra⁹ckelyng is . . . . . . . } xiiij*li.* xix*s.*

.ec̃ byJo.p. The Wholl Sum̃ of yᵉ Receyts of yᵉ forseyd Joħn Pers As is afore exp⁹ssed at yᵉ Accompts yᵉ yere pasteˑ . } v*li.*

In p⁹imis to Joħn Wodcoke for s⁹rten londs hyred of hym by the Chyrchewardēs frō yero to yere duryng his lease in ferme As is afore wrytte⁹ lyeng in the pasture . . . . . . } xix*s.* vj*d.*

Itm̃ for a Thalder of lyme bought at Walsynghm̃ . iiij*s.*

Itm̃ for yᵉ Caryeng therof frō thense to Elmhm̃ . . xx*d.*

Itm̃ payed to laborors when yᵉ dyggyng of Grauell was towards yᵉ mendyng of the lackyng monyc for yᵉʳ paynes, s. so moche As came to yᵉ Sum̃ of vij*d.*, &c. . . . . . . . . } vij*d.*

Itm̃ for A Chese for yᵉ Ryngers at Halowmes nyght . iiij*d.*

The Wholl Sum̃ of the Chargs of yᵉ seyd Joħn Peers is . . . . . . . . . . } xxvj*s.* ix*s.* j*d.*

In p⁹imis payed to yᵉ laborers & Caryers of Grauell towards yᵉ mendyng of yᵉ noysome wayes wᵗin Elmhm̃, fyrst of yᵉ gyfte of Rychard Pers now depted, iij*li.* vj*s.* viij*d.*; & of pte of yᵉ quethode ot M⁹ dethyke, xiij*s.* iiij*d.*; & yᵉ rest, wyche was viij*s.* iiij*d.*, was taken owt of yᵉ Town stock, &c. . . . . . . } iiij*li.* viij*s.* iiij*d.*

Itm̃ to Rychard Heyward att yᵉ Crosse for dyggyng of grauell iij dayes to yᵉ entents aforseyd . . . } xv*d.*

Itm̃ to yᵉ bekon watche for iij monethes . . . iij*s.*

Itm̃ to Lyngeyo for mendyng yᵉ wayes Aboue Jacks brydge & other, iij dayes, &c. . . . . } xij*d.*

Itm̃ to Joħn Wryght for a hēgell for A fallgate . . j*d.*

F

Itm̃ to Wyllm̃ Swāton for rydyng to Estderhm̃ ij tymes   ⎫
   for M⁹ Nowell concernyng serten busynes &  ⎬  viijd.
   makyng of wryghtyngs for yᵉ Town londs .  .  ⎭

Itm̃ to yᵒ seyd M⁹ Nowell for wryghtyng of sᵖrten  ⎫
   ynstrumēts coᵖcernyng yᵉ seyd lands, &c.  .  . ⎬  ijs.

Itm̃ in Expenss for hym & dyuᵖse other of yᵉ ynhabi-  ⎫
   tance of yᵉ Town, beyng pᵖsent at yᵉ seyd  ⎬  xviijd.
   busynes .  .  .  .  .  .  .  ⎭

Itm̃ for yᵉ fetchyng of A Sckyn of pchemēt from  ⎫
   Estderhm̃ .  .  .  .  .  .  . ⎬  ijd.

Itm̃ for ij C & d. of pauyng Tyle for yᵒ Chyrche.  .  vs.

Itm̃ for yᵉ Caryeng home therof & ij lods of Sonde  .  xviijd.

Itm̃ to Wyllm̃ ffyncke for layeng of yᵉ seyd Tyle in  ⎫
   dyuᵖse ptes of yᵒ Chyrche & Chapells, s. for ix  ⎬  iijs.  xjd.
   dayes worcke & d. afℭ vd. yᵉ daye.  .  .  .  ⎭

Itm̃ to hys sᵖuer viij dayes & d. afℭ iiijd. yᵉ daye.  .  ijs.  xd.

                   Sum̃, vli. xjs. iijd.

Itm̃ to yᵉ Cołour for yᵉ Leate ffee of yᵉ Londs in Betele xxiiijs.

Redᵗ solᵖ.  Itm̃ to hym for yᵉ rent of yᵉ Town Londs in Elmhm̃ .  vijs.

Itm̃ for yᵉ rent of yᵒ Town londs lyeng in Betele  .  vs.

Itm̃ to my Lady Hastyngs baly for rent yᵉʳ.  .  .  vjd.

Itm̃ to Wyllm̃ ffyncke for takyng down of sᵖtayn pancs  ⎫
   of Glasse in yᵉ Chyrche & Chapells & reparyng  ⎬  ixs.  iiijd.
   of yᵉᵐ .  .  .  .  .  .  .  .  ⎭

Itm̃ for one bʒ of Malte to be brown for yᵉ Ryngers at  ⎫
   Halowmes nyght .  .  .  .  .  . ⎬  vijd.

Itm̃ for halfe A bʒ of Whete to yᵉ seyd entent .  .  vd.

Itm̃ for yᵉ ffyeng of yᵉ pytt Vpon yᵉ gret heathe.  .  iijs.

Itm̃ to Wyllm̃ & he to Hewett of Worthyng for yᵉ  ⎫
   ffyeng of a drayn in Estagat, &c..  .  .  . ⎬  vd.

Itm̃ to Wyllm̃ yarrhm̃ for his ffee in tendyng &
trymyng yᵉ belles, &c. . . . . . }    xvj*d*.

Itm̃ to powls wyfe for yᵉ wasshyng of yᵉ Chyrche gere    xvj*d*.

Itm̃ to Wyllm̃ Tylney for hys fee, s. for yᵉ mēdyng of
the wyndowes in yᵉ Clerystoryes . . . . }    xij*d*.

Itm̃ to Herry Wells for tendyng of yᵉ bells . . .    vj*d*.

Itm̃ to yᵉ bekon watche the ij^{th} tyme for iij monēthes .    iij*s*.

Sum̃, lvij*s*. v*d*.

Itm̃ payed to Henry dyght for yᵉ ffyeng the pytt vpon
the grett heath one daye . . . . . }    iiij*d*.

Itm̃ payed to yᵉ bekon watche yᵉ iij^{th} tyme ij monethes    ij*s*.

Itm̃ payed for A Badrycke for yᵉ grett bell . . .    xij*d*.

Itm̃ in expens at ffakenhm̃ whē we were Co⁹mãded to
make A true s⁹tyfycat of all oʳ plate, Jewells,
ornamēts, Bells, & suche other . . . }    ij*s*.   vj*d*.

Itm̃ for yᵉ wryghtyng of oʳ s⁹tyfycat then . . .    iiij*d*.

Itm̃ to Wyllm̃ Tylneye for payntyng of yᵉ clothes
hangyng before yᵉ quere & the Sepulcre also, &c. . }    xiiij*d*.

Itm̃ to Barthrhm̃ for makyng yᵉ lectorn at yᵉ quere
dor . . . . . . . . }    iiij*d*.

Itm̃ for ij books & ij Sawlters for yᵉ order of the
new [65] sett forthe by the Kyngs Majesties Con̄ . }    xvj*s*. iiij*d*.

Itm̃ for iij books, beyng noted, Acordyng to yᵉ seyd
order . . . . . . . . }    iiij*s*.

Itm̃ in Expens at Lytchm̃ for oʳ Apperance yᵉʳ before
M⁹ Croke yᵉ Surueyoʳ to oʳ Sou⁹ayn Lorde Kyng
Edward yᵉ syxt of all Chantryes & suche other [66]. }    xij*d*.

Itm̃ to yᵉ bekon watche yᵉ iiij^{th} tyme, ij monethes .    ij*s*.

Itm̃ to Roger Hamond for yᵉ makyng of yᵉ pale at yᵉ
hethe Gat, fellyng of yᵉ Tymbre, &c. . . }    iij*s*. iiij*d*.

Itm̃ for yᵉ fall Gat ther, Tymber, ᵹ Worckmãˀshyp  .    xij*d.*

Itm̃ to Roƀt Barthm̃ for mendyng of yᵉ pales vpon yᵉ ⎫
northe syde of yᵉ Chyrchyard ᵹ yᵉ Style also yᵉʳ . ⎭  ij*s.*  vj*d.*

Itm̃ to herry wells for tending yᵉ Clocke  .    .    xij*d.*

Sum̃, **xxxviij***s.* **x***d.*

---

The wholl Sum̃ of yᵉ rec̃ of the seyd wyllm̃ ⎫
ffranckelyng, ys  .   .   .   .   . ⎭ xiiij*li.* xix*s.*

The Sum̃ of his Chargs ᵹ paymēts As is Afore- ⎫
seyd, is  .   .   .   .   .   . ⎭ x*li.* vij*s.* vj*d.*

ñ.    And so remayn in yᵉ hands of yᵉ seyd wyllm̃ As ⎫
is her leyd down at his Accompt, besyds all ⎮
thyngs payed, dyscharged, ᵹ due to be ⎬ iiij*li.* xj*s.* vj*d.*
rekened for his pte yᵉⁿ, is  .   .   . ⎭

The wholl Sum̃ of yᵉ rec̃ of yᵉ seyd John peers, is  v*li.*

The Sum̃ of his Chargs ᵹ paymēts, As is aforseyd, ⎫
is  .   .   .   .   .   .   . ⎭ xxvj*s.* j*d.*

ñ.    And so remayn in yᵉ hands of yᵉ seyd John, as is ⎫
her leyd down at his Accompt, besyds all ⎮
thyngs payed, dyscharged, ᵹ due to be ⎬ iij*li.* xiij*s.* xj*d.*
rekened for his pte yᵉⁿ, is  .   .   . ⎭

And so yᵉ seyd Wyllm̃ ffraˀckelyng ᵹ John pers ᵹ ⎫ et sic qˀeti sñt Aᵒ
yᵉʳ heyres be clerly dyscharged for thys yere ⎬
that ys paste, ᵹc.  .   .      . ⎭ pˀdict.

---

**Aᵒ Dm.**
**1550.**
**[Aᵒ 4ᵒ**
**Ed. VI.]**

Aᵒ dm̃. 1550ᵒ.

Mᵈ. A Rekenyng made vpon Trynyte Sondaye afᵗ Euynsong the
yere of oʳ lord god Mˡˡ ccccc ᵹ fyftye of wyllm̃ ffrackelyng ᵹ
henry Rustñ, Chyrchwardens of northelmhm̃ yᵉ samo ycre, ᵹc.

In pⁱimis delyuᵖed to yᵉᵐ at yᵉ Accompts, As is ⎫
   Aforseyd, s. Aᵒ dm̄ 1549ᵒ pᵖdictᵖ, viij*li.* vs. v*d.*, ⎪
   whereof remayn in yᵉ hands of the seyd ⎬ viij*li.*   vs.   v*d.*
   Wyllm̄ ffraᵖckelyng, iiij*li.* xjs. vj*d.*, ⱬ in the ⎪
   hands of herry Rustñ, yᵉ other Chyrch- ⎪
   warden, iij*li.* xiijs. xj*d.* .   .   .   . ⎭

Itm̄ rec̆ then by the seyd herry for londe fferme, s. of ⎫
   Nycholas purdye, xvj*d.*; of Hyᵖ selfe, ijs. iiij*d.*; ⎪
   wherof payed yᵉⁿ for wasshyng of yᵉ Chyrchegere ⎬ ijs.
   d. A yere, viij*d.*; to Tylneye for hys fee for ⎪
   reparyng of the Clerystoryes, xij*d.*; ⱬ so remayn ⎪
   in his hands of yᵉˢ last Sum̄s but .   .   . ⎭

Itm̄ rec̆ of herry Wakfelde for land fferme in yᵉ pasture   vjs.

Itm̄ rec̆ of John Wodcocke, ⱬc. .   .   .   .   iiij*d.*

Itm̄ rec̆ of Wyllm̄ Yarrhm̄ for lond fferme lyeng in ⎫
   Betele ⱬ Elmhm̄ due for yⁱˢ yere ⱬ other paste   .⎭ xljs.

Itm̄ rec̆ of Rob̆t Rudd of Betele for lond fferme yᵉʳ   .   xs.

Itm̄ rec̆ of John Marche of Bylney for lond fferme ⎫
   lyeng wⁱin yᵉ Townchype of Betele   .   .   .⎭ xiijs. iiij*d.*

Itm̄ rec̆ of Thom̄s Lussher for yᵉ Campyng Closse ⱬ ⎫
   other londs, lyeng in yᵉ ffylds of northelmhm̄   .⎭ vs. iiij*d.*

Itm̄ rec̆ of John Brow̄ measᵖ for lond fferme yᵉʳ   .   .   xv*d.*

Itm̄ rec̆ of Wyllm̄ Som̄e of Betele for lond ferme yᵉʳ   .   ijs. viij*d.*

      Sum̄, vij*li.* xvs. x*d.* s. rec̆ p h. R. pᵖ in toto pcen.

Itm̄ rec̆ of Rychard Man for londe fferme in Elmhm̄   .   ijs.

Itm̄ rec̆ for yᵉ Sett of the Comō lyght, Aulter Clothes, ⎫
   ⱬ sᵖten other thyngs solde ⱬ delyuᵖed in yᵉ pᵖsens ⎬ xxvs.
   of dyuᵖse of yᵉ pysshners yᵉʳ ⱬ then   .   .⎭

Itm̄ rec̆ of Wyllm̄ Euᵖode of Gatelee for londe fferme in ⎫
   yᵉ pasture of Elmhm̄   .   .   .   .   .⎭ vs.

Itm̃ reč of John Johnson of Bresole for lond fferme ⎱ xij*d*.
lyeng in his Closse at y^e heathe . . . . ⎰

Itm̃ reč of Herry Holme for y^e gret Anty-⎞ x*s*., but is now but
phoners, Grayles, Legends, Masbokes [67] ⎟ vj*s*. iiij*d*.,⅋ y^e rest was
⅋ all other kynds of boks of y^o olde s^9uyce, ⎟ Alowed hy^9 for lacke
x*s*., whereof reč to y^e Towns vse, ⅋ to ⎟ of hys wags y^t could
be rekened in myn Accompts, but ⎟ not be gathered in
vj*s*. iiij*d*. . . . . . . . ⎠ Town, ⅋c.

Sum̃, xxxix*s*. iiij*d*.

The wholl Sum̃e of y^e Reyceyts of y^e seyd Herry ⎱ y*s* ixl*i*. xv*s*. ij*d*.
Ruston the yere that is paste . . . ⎰

Paymẽts by the seyd Herry Rustñ, ⅋c., ut seq̃.

In p^9imis to y^e lords Colour for y^e let fet (*sic*) of y^e ⎱ xxiiij*s*.^a
Town londs, both of Elmhm̃ ⅋ Betele . . . ⎰

Rcd^t sol^9. Itm̃ for y^o Rent of y^e Town londs of Elmhm̃ . . vij*s*.
Itm̃ for y^o Rent of y^e said Town londs in Betele . . v*s*.
Itm̃ for s^9ten londs lyeng w^tin Elmhm̃ And Betele ⎱ vj*s*.
payeng Rent to y^e Chapell of y^e Becke [68] . ⎰
Itm̃ to my Lady Hastyngs Baly for Rent . . . vj*d*.
Itm̃ to Herry wells for tendyng y^e bells . . . vj*d*.
Itm̃ to Herry Swanton for ffyrckyngs . . . . xv*d*.
Itm̃ to Clercks wyffe for A mat to lye befor y^e Table ⎱ iij*d*.
of y^o Lord to knele on. . . . . . ⎰
Itm̃ to Hugh pye for hedgyng of y^e Town Carre, lyeng ⎱ xvj*d*.
w^tin y^e p^9cyncte of Betele [69] . . . . ⎰
Itm̃ payod for nayles to mend w^t y^e stocks [70] . . j*d*.
Itm̃ for ij plancks to mend w^t payforde brydge . . viij*d*.
Itm̃ to Wyllm̃ Smythe for y^o Bekon watche . ij*s*.

Itm̃ to yᵉ seyd Wyllm̃ towarde yᵉ settyng forthe of yᵉ ⎫
Soudyours of northelmhm̃ ɞ other [71]  .  .  . ⎭ vs.

Sum̃, liijs. vijd.

ñ. The sum̃es of monye payed ɞ delyuᵖed by me yᵉ seyd Herry Ruston
in yᵉ tyme of yᵉ Campe at Mussolde wᵗ yᵉ Assent ɞ consent of
the ynhabytañce of yᵉ Townchype of Elmhm̃, ɞ wherfore ɞ to
whom, As heraft in ther pcells more plynly shall Apere, ɞc.

In pᵒimis to John Wryght for to bye wᵗ one ffyrkyng ⎫
of beare, ɞ for yᵉ Gage of yᵉ ffyrkyng .  .  . ⎭ xvjd.

Itm̃ for ffysshe, xijd.; for bred, vjd.; for Musterd, ijd.; ⎫
for Garlecke ɞ Oynnyngs bought yᵉʳ ɞ theᵖ, ijd. . ⎭ xxijd.

Itm̃ to wyllm̃ dycks for hys Cart ɞ Horses to Cary wᵗ ⎫
vytalls to the seyd Campe  .  .  .  . ⎭ ijs.

Itm̃ delyuᵖed to Thom̃s powle, my ptener yᵉⁿ, to be ⎫
bestowed vpon suche thyngs as yᵉʳ neaded  . ⎭ vjs. viijd.

Itm̃ delyuᵖed to hyᵖ aft yᵗ to yᵉ entents aforseyd .  . xvjd.

Itm̃ Alowed to my selffe for my Carte ɞ Horses to cary ⎫
wᵗ vytalls to yᵉ seyd Campe, ɞc.  .  .  . ⎭ ijs.

Itm̃ for bred yᵉⁿ, vjd.; for iij ffyrkyngs of bere yᵉⁿ, ijs.vjd. iijs.

Itm̃ for bred aft yᵗ, iiijd. And delyuᵖed also to yᵉ seyd ⎫
Thom̃s powle, my ptener, to yᵉ entents aforseyd, ⎬ iiijs. iiijd.
iiijs. .  .  .  .  .  .  .  . ⎭

Itm̃ payed to dycks wyff aft yᵗ for j fyrckyng of Alle, ⎫
xd.; for ffysshe yᵉⁿ, viijd.; for Salt yᵉⁿ, ijd. . ⎭ xxd.

Itm̃ to Thom̃s pettus for ij Saulter bokes  .  .  . vs. iiijd.

Sum̃, xxixs. vjd.

Itm̃ Alowed to my selffe for my Carte ɞ Horses aft yᵗ ⎫
to Carye wᵗ vytalls to yᵉ seyd Campe, ɞc.  . ⎭ ijs.

Itm̃ for yᵉ Repacon of yᵒ Hernes, vj*d*. oƀ; for Arow
Heads, j*d*.; for bred, vj*d*.; for oynyngs, j*d*.; for
bredd afᵗ yᵗ, xiij*d*.; for Arowes, ij*d*.; for Halters,   iiij*s*. viij*d*.
ij*d*.; for bredd, ij*d*.; for ij fyrkyngs of bere, xx*d*.;    & j*d*.
to Thom̃s Tott for meᵖdy̆g of his bowe & stryngs,
iij*d*. oƀ  .  .  .  .  .  .  .  .  .  .

Itm̃ for bredd afᵗ yᵗ, v*d*.; to Motts for ij Staues, vj*d*.;
for oynyngs, j*d*. oƀ; to pytcher for j staff, iij*d*.;   iiij*d*. x*d*. oƀ
for iiij ffyrkyngs of bere, iij*s*. iiij*d*.; for butter, j*d*.;
ffor bredd to John Bawett, ij*d*.  .  .  .  .

Sum̃, xjs. vijd. oƀ.

Itm̃ to Herry wakfeld for meᵖdyng of hys Hernes, j*d*.;   ix*d*.
for bred, vj*d*.; for bredd afᵗ yᵗ, ij*d*.  .  .

Itm̃ Alowed to my selffe for my wags & pt of my
Com̃ons, xxj*d*.; for j fyrkyng of bere, x*d*.; for   iij*s*. viij*d*.
bredd, iiij*d*.; for ffyssh, viij*d*.; for tack nayles, j*d*.  .

Itm̃ Alowed to my selffe for my Carte & Horses after
yᵗ to Cary wᵗ vytalls to yᵉ seyd Campe, &c.  .  .   ij*s*.

Itm̃ to Herry Wakfelde & Clemēt Gnoo for yᵒʳ expᵖess,
& of yᶜʳ horses in norwᶜʰ, when they caryed yᵉ
Meale & Malte, xx*d*.; for Salt & bredd, iiij*d*.; for   ij*s*. iiij*d*.
ffysshe & Oynyngs, iij*d*.  And for yᵉ brewyng of
one ffyrkyng of ber, wᵗin norwyche, j*d*.  .  .

Itm̃ in Expenss at ffuckehm̃ for Mᵖ vycar And other
Coᵖmāded to be before yᵉ kyngs Coᵖmyssyoncrs   xxij*d*.
yᵒʳ ⁽⁷²⁾  .  .  .  .  .  .  .  .  .

Sum̃, xs. vijd.

Itm̃ in Expenss at ffukehm̃ afᵗ yᵗ for Masᵗ vycare and
other Commanded to Aper before my lord of   ij*s*. iij*d*.
Canterburyes vysitors, &c.  .  .  .  .  .

Itm̃ to wyllm̃ ffyncke j day to helpe to pull down the ⎫
Aulter for hys wags ꝛ Com̃ons yᵉ seyd daye .   . ⎭ nˡⁱ·* ꝛc.

Itm̃ Alowed to my selffe for me ꝛ my ij men one day ⎫
pullyng down yᵉ seyd Aulters for wags ꝛ Com̃ons . ⎭ xviijd.

Itm̃ Alowed to my selffe for ij dayes ꝛ d. for me ꝛ my ⎫
men takyng down yᵉ backe of yᵉ hye Aulter⁽⁷³⁾      ⎪
And settyng vp ꝛ trymyng of yt in yᵉ myds of yᵉ ⎬ ijs.   vjd.
quier, ꝛc.   .       .       .       .       .       .       . ⎭

Itm̃ for yᵉ Tymbre for the seyd Aulter .     .     .       xd.
Itm̃ for nayles for yᵉ seyd Aulter ꝛ yᵉ Vestrye dore   .       ijd.
Itm̃ to yᵉᵐ that toke down yᵉ Aulter stone .     .     iiijd.
Itm̃ for yᵉ mendyng of A mattocke yᵗ was broke⁹     .       ijd.
Itm̃ to John wodcocke for land fferme in yᵉ pasture   .   xixs.   vjd.
Itm̃ to Herry Holme for lacs for yᵉ Saulter boks And ⎫
yᵉ other boks of s⁹uyce now onlye vsed,⁽⁷⁴⁾ ꝛc.   . ⎭ ijd.

Itm̃ to Wyllm̃ Tylney for yᵉ whyghtyng of y° seyd ⎫
new Aulter ꝛ y° mynystryng Table therof   .   . ⎭ ixd.

Itm̃ to Wyllm̃ Smyth towards yᵉ settyng furth ⎫
of yᵉ Sowdyours of Landytcher Hu⁹dered, ꝛc. ⎭ iiijs. xjd. ꝛ ijd.

Itm̃ leyd ought at Lytchm̃ for M⁹ vycare ꝛ other whe⁹ ⎫
we wer Com̃anded ther to Apere. And to bryng    ⎪
yn all yᵉ bokes of yᵉ olde s⁹uyce⁽⁷⁵⁾ ꝛ for y°  ⎬ xiijd.
wryghtyng of yᵉ Certyfycat of yᵉᵐ, ꝛc.   .     . ⎭

Sum̃, xxxiiijs. iiijd.

Itm̃ reč of Thom̃s Shetell for londe ferme .     .     . iiijs.   ijd.

ñ.      Wherof was Alowed to hym for Caryeng of vytalls to ⎫
yᵉ Campe at norwyche .     .     .     .     . ⎭ ijs.

The wholl Sum̃e of yᵉ Cargs (sic) ꝛ paymets of ⎫
yᵉ seyd Henry Rustm̃ for yᵉ yere yᵗ is past ⎭ ys, vjlⁱ. xixs. vijd. ꝋ

* I imagine that "n " is here equivalent to " nil," meaning that no money entry
was made. It is not included in the sum total at the foot of the account, which is
correct without it.—A. G. L.

ñ p⁹.

Paymēts by the seyd Wyllm̃ ffra⁹ckelyng, &c., ut seq̃.

In p⁹imis to Rychard Purdy for Caryeng of Grauell ⎫
to mend wᵗ Byllyngforde brydge . . . . ⎭    xijd.

Itm̃ to tweyn plum̃ers j daye & d. for ther wags & ⎫
Com̃ons the seyd tyme . . . . . . ⎭   ijs.

Itm̃ payed to them for vijᵘ of Powder . . . .   iiijs.   ijd.

Itm̃ Alowed to my selffe for wood spent yᵉⁿ . . .    iiijd.

ñ. p⁹. seq̃.   Itm̃ delyũed to those of yᵉ Townchype of Elmhm̃ yᵗ ⎫
went ffyrst to yᵉ Campe at Mussholde, that ys to ⎪
seye, to xij of the⁹, by the Assent and Consent of ⎪
yᵉ seyd Townchype, besyds other Chargs yᵉʳ, by ⎬   xijs.
yᵉ seyd Assent and Consent, As heraftʳ in yᵉʳ ⎪
seuᵒall pcells, wherfor and to whom they wer ⎪
payed & delyu⁹ed, more playnly shall Aper, &c. ⎭

Itm̃ to yᵉ wyues of Herry ffyld & Robt Clerk yᵉ seyd ⎫
tyme, pore folcks, yᵉʳ husbonds beyng at yᵉ Campe ⎭   viijd.

Itm̃ delyu⁹ed afℓ yᵗ to s⁹ten of yᵉ seyd Town goyng to ⎫
yᵉ seyd Campe, s. for yᵉʳ Expenss by the waye . ⎭   ijs.

Itm̃ to Rychard Watson & hys Compenye afℓ yᵗ for yᵉʳ ⎫
expenss also, by yᵉ waye thyther . . . . ⎭   viijd.

Itm̃ to Thom̃s Wakfeld afℓ yᵗ toward yᵉ healyng of hys ⎫
hand & fface, hurt at yᵉ ffyrst skyrmyssh, &c. . ⎭   xijd.

Itm̃ payed yᵉ xᵗʰ daye of Auguste to suche as shold ⎫
tarye at the seyd Campe for yᵉʳ wags one weke, ⎬ xiiijs.
that is to seye, to Eyght of yᵉᵐ, wᵗ yᵉ Constable . ⎭

Itm̃ for mendyng of Hernes yᵉʳ, vjd.; & to one yᵗ ⎫
turned yᵉ Spets, ijd.; for ffysshe, iiijd.; to Brown ⎬   xvjd.
yᵉ la. (? labourer) yᵉʳ also, iiijd. . . . . ⎭

Itm̃ to Roḃt Clercke then for hys wags one monethe
beyng y<sup>er</sup> Coke, besyds y<sup>e</sup> gyfte to hys wyf Afore } iijs. iiijd.
wrytt<sup>9</sup> .

Suñ, xlijs. vjd.

Itm̃ delyṽed to y<sup>em</sup> of y<sup>e</sup>Campe the xiiij daye of Auguste }
aft̃ y<sup>t</sup> for s̃<sup>9</sup>ten thyngs to be bought y<sup>er</sup> & then . } xs.

Itm̃ to Lamberd for byeng of ffysshe & other Chargs }
for hym & his horse the Saterday & Sonday aft̃ y<sup>t</sup> } xvjd.

Itm̃ delyṽed to Thom̃s Powle, one of the Constables }
of northelmhm̃ at y<sup>e</sup> same tyme, &c. . . . } iijs. iiijd.

Itm̃ payed to viij men y<sup>e</sup> xx<sup>ti</sup> daye of August aft̃ y<sup>t</sup>, }
w<sup>ch</sup> wer Apoynted to tery y<sup>er</sup>, for y<sup>er</sup> wags, aft̃ iijd. } xiiijs.
y<sup>o</sup> daye.

Itm̃ to vj men y<sup>t</sup> Came from y<sup>o</sup> Campe then to dryncke }
w<sup>t</sup> homeward by the waye, &c. . . . . } vjd.

Itm̃ to y<sup>o</sup> Turner of y<sup>e</sup> Spets, ijd. And sent to y<sup>o</sup> }
Campe y<sup>o</sup> Twysdaye next aft̃ y<sup>t</sup> by John Wryght, } xs. ijd.
xs.

Itm̃ to Handforthe & hys sone for y<sup>o</sup> Caryeng of one }
barrell of bere to y<sup>e</sup> seyd Campe on horse backe . } xijd.

huc ñ. Itm̃ delyṽed to Thom̃s Tott y<sup>e</sup> Saterday befor y<sup>e</sup> last
Skyrmysshe for hy<sup>9</sup> & hys Co<sup>9</sup>penye for to dryncke } xiiijd.
w<sup>t</sup> by the waye, &c. . . . . .

Itm̃ to s̃<sup>9</sup>ten of y<sup>e</sup> pysshe for y<sup>e</sup> takyng down of y<sup>e</sup> }
bells, xijd., & to Roḃt Barthra<sup>9</sup> for hys Tacle y<sup>en</sup>, ijd. } xiiijd.

Itm̃ to Lyngey for me<sup>9</sup>dyng of y<sup>e</sup> fence of y<sup>e</sup> Chyrch
yerde Ageÿst Margarett Reyners Gard<sup>9</sup>, ijd. And }
to Wyllm̃ Smythe towards A falgate in Sellew } xiiijd.
Lane, xijd. . . . . . .

Suñ, xliijs. xd.

The wholl Suم̃e of y$^e$ Reč of y$^e$ seyd Wyllm̃ | iiij*li.*   xj*s.*  vj*d.*
ffra$^9$ckylyng ys  .  .  .  .  .  .  . }

The Suم̃e of hys Chargs & paymēts, As aforseyd, ys iiij*li.* vj*s.* iiij*d.*

And so remayn in hys hands, As ys her leyd downe at ⎫
his Acompts, all thyngs dyscharged, due to be ⎬  v*s.*  ij*d.*
rekened y$^{en}$ .  .  .  .  .  .  . ⎭

Thc wholl suم̃e of y$^e$ reč of y$^e$ seyd Herry Rustñ, ys, ix*li.* xv*s.* ij*d.*

The Suم̃e of his Chargs & paymēts, As aforseyd, ys, vj*li.* xix*s.* vij*d.*

And so remayn in his hands, As is her leyd downe at ⎫
his Accompts, all thyngs dyscharged, due to be ⎬  l*s.* vj*d.* oƀ
rekened y$^{en}$ .  .  .  .  .  .  .  . ⎭

And so y$^o$ (seyd) Wyllm̃ ffrankelyng & Herry Ruston, And ther
heyres, be clerly dyscharged for y$^{ts}$ yere that is paste, &c. Et sic
q$^9$eti sñt A$^o$ p̃.

A$^o$ Dm.               A$^o$ dm̃ 1551$^o$.
1551.      M$^d$. A Rekenyng mad vpon Trynyte Sondaye aft̃ Eũesonge, the yer of
[A$^n$ 5$^o$     o$^r$ Lord M$^{ll}$ccccc & ffyftye & one, of Herry Rustñ & Rychard
Edw. VI.]  ffranckelyng, Chyrchewardens y$^{ts}$ yere comyng, &c.

In p$^9$imis delyũed to y$^{em}$ at y$^e$ Accompts, the yere of o$^r$ ⎫
lord god, M$^{ll}$ccccc & ffyftye afore seyd, s. in y$^e$ |
hands of Herry Rustñ Aforseyd all the$^9$ due to be |
payed, s. to Herry Wells for y$^e$ Clooke, xij*d.*; to ⎬ iij*li.* xviij*d.* oƀ
Tylney for repayng of y$^e$ Clerystoryes, xij*d.* And |
so remayn in hys hands  .  .  .  .  . ⎭

Itm̃ reč y$^{en}$ for lond ferme due then & before, ix*s.* viij*d.*; ⎫
s. of Edmñde ffletcher, iiij*s.*; Wyllm̃ ffranckelyng, |
xij*d.*; of Nycholas purdye, xvj*d.*; of Herry Rustñ, |
ij*s.* iiij*d.*; of Rychard Rustñ, xij*d.*; wherof payed for ⎬ vj*s.*  viij*d.*
wasshyng of y$^o$ Chyrche gere, xvj*d.*; & to Tylney for |
ij locks, viij*d.*; to s$^9$ John Elũyche for wryghtyng |
of y$^e$ Accompts & dyũse other thyngs, xij*d.* And so |
remayn in hys hands of y$^e$ seyd receyts, ut suƥ, &c. ⎭

Itm̃ reč of Thom̃s Marche of Bylneye for land fferme longyng to northelmhm̃ . . . . . } xiijs. iiij*d.*

Itm̃ reč of Robt Rud of Betele for lande ferme . . xs.

Itm̃ reč of Wyllm Yarrhm̃ for yᵉ Town Closse · . xxs.

Itm̃ reč of Rychard Crow for land fferme . . . iijs. iiij*d.*

Itm̃ reč of Hugh Peryman for land ferme . . . xij*d.*

Itm̃ reč of Thom̃s Lussher for yᵉ Campyng closse . iijs. iiij*d.*

Itm̃ reč of Wyllm̃ Rudd for land ferme . . . x*d.*

Itm̃ reč of Rychard Ruston for land fferme . . . viij*d.*

Itm̃ reč of Nycholas Purdy for land fferme . . . x*d.*

Itm̃ reč of Wyllm̃ Ẽgrym for land fferme . . . viij*d.*

Itm̃ reč of dyũse other for land ferme lyeng wᵗin Elmhm̃ & Betele, s. Thom̃s Clercke, vj*d.*; of John Browᷓ meas⁹, xij*d.*; of Wyllm̃ Sohm̃ of Betele, ijs. viij*d.*; of Thom̃s Powle, xij*d.*; of John Johnson of Bresele, xij*d.*; of Herry ffylde, ix*d.*; of Wyllm̃ } xijs. ij*d.* Smythe, iiij*d.*; of Wyllm̃ Tho⁹pson, husbondmā, xij*d.*; of Edward Handforde, x*d.*; of Thom̃s Shetell, xij*d.*; of Symond Shetell, xij*d.*; of Wyllm̃ ffranckelyng, xiij*d.* . . . . . . /

Sum̃, vj*li.* xiijs. viij*d.* oƀ.

Itm̃ reč for yᵉ olde Ault⁹, yᵉ Sepulcre, And s⁹ten other olde thyngs Afor Acustomed to be occupyed in } viijs. vj*d.* the Chyrche, in yᵉ tyme of yᵉ s⁹uys then . .

Itm̃ reč of Rychard Pytcher for land ferme, x*d.*; of Herry Wakfelde, vjs.; of Edmñde ffletcher, iiijs.; of Rychard Ruston xvj*d.*; of Ry. ffra⁹kelyng, } xixs. ij*d.* ijs. vj*d.*; of Herry Ruston, iiijs. vj*d.* . . .

Itm̃ reč of John Wryght for s⁹ten olde yron . . xvj*d.*

Itm̃ reč of dyks wyfe for An·olde bañer clothe   .    .     vj*d*.

Sum̃, xxixs. vjd.

Itm̃ reč of Rychard ffranckelyng ⁊ Hugh Perymā for � ij small ooks ⁊ yᵉ Topps of them  .   .   .   .   ij*s*. viij*d*.

Sum̃ Total p̃cedens, viijli. vs. xd. oƀ.

Rent of the town londs.

Paym̃ẽts by the seyd Henry Ruston<br>⁊ Rychard ffrākelyng—

In p̃ᵒimis payed to Robt Lussher towards yᵉ mendyng of yᵉ falgate in Westfelde, ⁊c.  .  .  .  .   iiij*d*.

Itm̃ to Mᵖ Quayts for hys hayer yᵉ wyᶜʰ we had [at] yᵉ Campe ⁊ was loste ther, ⁊c.  .  .  .  .   iij*s*. iiij*d*.

Itm̃ to John Wryght for worke of his occupacon At the ynstance of Good man ffrākelyng, ⁊c.  .  .   xvij*d*.

Itm̃ for A payer of Stocks [76] to punysshe wᵗ tra⁹sgressours Ageynste yᵒ Kyngs Maiesties Lawes, ⁊c.  .  .  .  .  .   iij*s*. iiij*d*.

Itm̃ to yᵉ Lords Colour for yᵉ leate fee of Elmhm̃  .   xxiiij*s*.

**Elmhm̃.**   Itm̃ to Hyᵍ for yᵉ Rent of yᵒ Town Lands yᵉʳ  .   vij*s*.—iij*s*. vj*d*.

**Betele.**   Itm̃ to yᵉ balye for Rent of yᵉʳ lands in Betele  .   v*s*.—ij*s*. vj*d*.

**Reddit solut.**   Itm̃ to James Lynne of Norwyche for a Copper Sthetell, A Spete, ⁊ A Payle loste at yᵒ Campe   x*s*. ij*d*.

**ñ.**
**To yᵉ becke.**   Itm̃ to Robt Peper for Rent of s̃ten lands lyeng wᵗin Elmhm̃, ⁊c., ⁊ paye Rente to yᵒ Chapell of yᵉ becke  .  .  .  .   vj*s*.

Itm̃ to Wyllm̃ ffyncke for mendyng of yᵉ glasse wyndow of yᵉ Chyrche dore on yᵉ south syde  .  .   iij*s*. viij*d*.

Itm̃ to hy⁹ for fyllyng of s⁹ten holes in yᵉ walls of the } xijᵈ.
Chansell, &c.⁽⁷⁷⁾ . . . . . . . }

Itm̃ to my Lady Hastyngs balye for Rent . . . vjᵈ.

Sum̃, iijˡⁱ. vs. ixᵈ. oƀ.

Itm̃ in Expenss at Walsynghm̃ whan we wer Co⁹manded }
to Apere before the bysshops Vysytours, & for oʳ } xviijᵈ.
Certyfycat yᵉʳ . . . . . . }

Itm̃ for yᵉ setyng of A longe forme ⁽⁷⁸⁾ stondyng in yᵉ } ijᵈ.
cha⁹sell for to syt vpon in yᵉ tyme of yᵉ Co⁹munyo⁹ }

Itm̃ to Symond Blomefelde for one lood of wodd for }
Mother Sand⁹, vjᵈ., & to Egrym for yᵉ Caryeng } xᵈ.
yᵉʳof, iiijᵈ. . . . . . . . }

Itm̃ for yᵉ Mynystryng Table in the Quyere, &c. . . iiijs. viijᵈ.

Itm̃ for A falgat at yᵉ northe pt of yᵉ gret hethe, & for } ijs. iiijᵈ.
A Stulppe ⁽⁷⁹⁾ therto, & yᵉ Caryeng of them . . }

Itm̃ for Hoks And Verdells ⁽⁸⁰⁾ for yᵉ seyd Gate . . viijᵈ.

Itm̃ to John wodcoke for s⁹ten lands heyred of hym & } xixs. vjᵈ.
lyeng in yᵉ pastur⁹ of yᵉ northe fylde, &c. . . }

Itm̃ for yᵉ Carpet Cloth yᵗ lyeth vpon yᵉ Mynystryng }
Table . . . . . . . . } vs.

Itm̃ to Rychard Tylney for Castyng & whyghtyng yᵉ }
wall wher yᵉ Hey Ault⁹ was before, &c.. . . } iiijᵈ.

Sum̃, xxxvs.

Itm̃ to Wyllm̃ Tylneye for hys yerly ffee for reparyng } xijᵈ.
of yᵉ Clerystoryes of yᵉ Chyrche . . . . }

Itm̃ to Herry Wells for his fee to tend yᵉ Clooke . . xijᵈ.

Itm̃ to powls wyffe for wasshyng of yᵉ Chyrche Gere }
& makyng yᵉ Syrples, iiijᵈ. . . . . . } xijᵈ. & iiijᵈ.

Sum Total p⁹cedens, vˡⁱ. iiijs. jᵈ. oƀ.

The wholl suṁe of yᵉ Rꝺ of yᵉ seyd Herry Rustñ  
    & Rychard ffranckelyng for the yere ⎬ viij*li*. v*s*. x*d*. oƀ  
    Afforseyd, ys  .   .   .   .   .

The wholl suṁe of yᵉʳ Chargs yᵉ seyd yere, ys  .   v*li*. iiij*s*. j*d*. oƀ

And so remayn in ther hands, As her ys layde  
    down at yᵉʳ Accompts, All thyngs dyscharged ⎬ iij*li*.         xxj*d*.  
    due then to be rekened & payed  .   .

And so yᵉ seyd Herry Rustñ & Rychard ffranckelyng & yᵉʳ heyres be  
clerly dyscharged for thys yere paste.  Et sic q᷎eti sñt A᷉ ꝑ.

A᷉ dṁ. 1552.

Mᵈ. A Rekenyng made vpon Trynyte Sondaye aftᵉ Eue᷎songe, the  
yere of oʳ lord god Mᴵᴵccccc lijᵗⁱ of Rychard ffra᷎ckelyng & Edmñd  
ffletcher, Chyrche Wardens thys yere comyng.

In p᷎imis delyꝟed to yᵉᵐ at yᵉ Accompts the yere  
    of oʳ Lord Mᴵᴵccccc fyfty & one Aforseyd, All ⎬ iij*li*.         xx*d*.  
    thyngs due to be payed then    .   .

Itṁ they reꝯ yᵉⁿ of John Pers for yᵉ legacye of ⎬ iij*li*.  vj*s*.  viij*d*.  
    Rychard Pers, late hys ffather  .   .

            Suṁ, vj*li*. viij*s*. iiij*d*.

| | | | |
|---|---|---|---|
| Receyts for ferme londe in Beteley & Elmham. | It. reꝯ of Thomas Marche of bylney for londe ferme longyne to Elmham | xiij*s*. | iiij*d*. |
| | It. reꝯ of Robert Rudde for londe ferme | x*s*. | |
| | It. reꝯ of Rychard Crowe for londe ferme | iij*s*. | iiij*d*. |
| | It. reꝯ of Hugh Perymane for lande ferme | xij*d*. | |
| | It. reꝯ of Thomas Lusshe᷎ for yᵉ campynge closse | iij*s*. | iiij*d*. |
| Reꝯ for fermeloude in clmhame | It. reꝯ of Wyllṁ Rudde for ferme lande | x*d*. | |
| | It. reꝯ of Rycharde Rustone for ferme londe | viij*d*. | |
| | It. reꝯ of Nycholas Purdy for ferme lande | x*d*. | |

It. rec̃ of Wyllm̃ Egryme for ferme lande . . . viijd.

It. rec̃ of othe⁹ diue⁹sse for lande ferme lyyng w'in
Elmham ⱬ Betele, s. Thomas clercke, vjd.; of John
Browne Meas⁹, xijd.; of Thomas Chome of Beteley,
ijs. viijd.; of Thomas Powle, xijd.; of John John-
sone of Beteley, xijd.; of Henrye fylde, ixd.; of
Wyllm̃ Smythe, iiijd.; of Wyllm̃ Tompsone,
Husbonde man, xijd.

Sum̃, xlijs. iijd.

It. of Edwarde Hanforde, xd.; of Thomas Shettell, xijd.;
of Symone Shettell, xijd.; of Wyllm̃ franckelyng,
xijd.

ec̃ for   It. rec̃ of Rychard Pytchar for lande ferme, xd.; of
nd ferme   Henry Wakefelde, vjs.; of Edmunde Fletche⁹,
Elmham   iiijs.; of Rycharde Rustone, xvjd.; of Rychard
francklynge, ijs. vjd.; of Henry Rustone, iiijs. vjd.

Sum̃, xxiijs.

ñ. Sum̃ Total p⁹ced, Rec̃, ixli. xiijs. vijd.

The sum̃e of the losse of yᵉ Rec̃ Aforseyd by the ffalls of yᵉ monye [81]
yᵗ yere ys ls. xjd. And so remayn in yᵉ Chyrchewardens hands
wᵗ yᵉʳ Allowance of yᵉ payments yᵗ folowe dew to be rekened
for, but iijli. xijs. As followethe At yᵉ end of yᵉʳ Accompts, Hoc
sig̃. ✝, &c.

Payments by yᵉ seyde Rycharde franckelynge ⱬ Edmund Fletcher yᵉ
yeare of oʳ lord god M°cccclij^ti.

It. payde to yᵉ Chappell at yᵉ Becke . . . . vjs.
It. pᵈ to John Lambert for paylyng in yᵉ chyrch yearde ⎫
of yᵉ northe pte . . . . . . . ⎬ iijs. iiijd.

G

It. to Robert Lussher for fersyng at yᵉ hethe . . xiij*d*.

It. to Henry Wells for feyyng of yᵉ gratte . . . ij*d*.

It. for ij chalder of lyme . . . . . . x*s*. viij*d*.

Su͂m, **xxj***s*. ij*d*.

It. for yᵉ emendyng of yᵉ dreyne at thornwell . . viij*d*.

It. to Henry Rustone for emendyng of a faldgaate at }
the hethe . . . . . . . . . } vj*d*.

Edmunde Fletcher begynethe here.

Redd' soluᵗ { It. for lete fee . . . . . . . . . xxiiij*s*.

Elmham.   It. for Rente of yᵉ Towne lande . . . . vij*s*.

Beteley.   It. for yᵉ Rente of yᵉ lands in beteley . . . . v*s*.

It. pᵈ to Wyllͫ Purdy for yᵉ chyrchgaat makyng . x*d*.

It. pᵈ Rente to my lady Hastyngs . . . . vj*d*.

It. to Johne Wryghte for hooks & hangles for yᵉ gatte . xvj*d*.

It. to yᵉ same John for a plaate for a stoole in yᵉ chyrche j*d*.

It. to John Lamberd for mendyng of yᵉ Rayles by sor }
(? Sir) Thomas Stephesone doore . . . . } iiij*d*.

It. to John Browne for castynge yᵉ lyme in to yᵉ porche ij*d*.

It. to Robert Clercke for castynge of v loode sonde . vj*d*.

It. Wyllͫ hers & Robert Clercke for qwenchynge of the }
lyme . . . . . . . . . . } xij*d*.

It. to Symone dymunde for caryynge of ij chaulder of }
lyme . . . . . . . . . . } vj*s*. iiij*d*.

It. to Wyllͫ Egrym for v loode of sonde . . . xv*d*.

Suͫm,                   Suͫma toˡˡˢ p'dict exspes'.
xlix*s*. vj*d* The wholle sͫme of yᵉ Rec' of yᵉ seyd Rychard }
Francklyng & Edmͥde fletche' for yeare } ix*li*. xiij*s*. vij*d*.
aforeseyde . . . . . . }

The wholle suṁe of yᵉ charges yᵉ seyde yeare .    iij*li.* x*s.* viij*d.*

ıı. p⁹. ✛    The suṁe of yᶜ lose of yᶜ Reċ aforseyd by the ⎱
falls of yᵉ monye yᵗ yere is . . . ⎰    l*s.* xj*d.*

And so Remayne in yᵉʳ hands as her is layde⎫
downe at ther accownts all thyngs dys-⎪
charged ⅋ due yᵉⁿ to be reckened and⎬ iij*li.* xij*s.*
payed ys but . . . . . ⎭

And so yᵉ seyd Rychard Francklynge ⅋ Edmunde Fletcher ⅋ yᵉʳ
heyers be clerly dyscharged for yᵉ yer past.

---

A° Dm.                A° dṁ. 1553.
1553.    Mᵈ. A Rekenyng made vpon yᵉ feast of yᵉ Natyuyte of Seaynt Joħn
ı° 7° Edw.    Baptyste yᶜ yeare of oʳ lord god Mᶜcccccliijᵗˡ of Edmunde
[. & 1°    fletcher ⅋ Wyllṁ Tompsone, Chyrche Wardens thys yere.
Mary.]    In p⁹imis delyuered to yᵉᵐ at yᵉ accompts yᵉ yere of oʳ ⎫
N. P'.    lord Mˡˡcccccliijᵗˡ afor wrytten, all thyngs due the⁹ ⎬iij*li.* xij*s.*
to be payed . . . . . . . . ⎭
And so eyche of yᵉᵐ reċ        . . . xxxvj*s.*
Suṁ, iij*li.* xij*s.*

---

ñ.    Reċ for lande fferme longyng to yᵉ Townchype of Northelmhṁ, ⅋c.,
lyeng wᵗin yᶜ Town ⅋ fyldes ther And Betelee, ut in pcells seq̃.
In p⁹imis of Thoṁs Lussher for yᵉ Campyng closse . iij*s.* iiij*d.*
Itṁ of Thoṁs Marche for londe fferme, xiij*s.* iiij*d.*; of⎫
Roḃt Rudd, x*s.*; of Rychard Crowe, iij*s.* iiij*d.*; of⎪
Wyllṁ Shom, ij*s.* viij*d.*; of Wyllṁ Thompson,⎪
xij*d.*; of Wyllṁ Rudd, xij*d.*; of Edward Hand-⎬xxxvj*s.* vij*d.*
forde, x*d.*; of Thoṁs Powell, xij*d.*; of Nycholas⎪
Purdye, x*d.*; of Wy̋tt ffra⁹ckelyng, xiij*d.*; of Wyllṁ⎪
Egrym, viij*d.*; of Joħn Joħnson, xij*d.* . . ⎭
Suṁ, xxxix*s.* xj*d.*

Itm̃ of Wyllm̃ Smythe, iiij*d.*; of Herry ffylde, ix*d.*; of⎫
John Brown meas⁹, xij*d.*; of Rychard Pytcher, ⎪
x*d.*; of Rychard Ruston, viij*d.*; of Symon Shetell ⎪
for yᵉ Town Closse, xx*s.*, ɀ for lande fferme, xx*d.*; ⎬xxvij*s.*  iij*d.*
of Thom̃s Shetell, xij*d.*; of Hugh Peryma⁹ for ⎪
A busshye pytell, xij*d.* .     .     .     .     .⎭

Sum̃, xxvij*s.* iij*d.*

ñ.   Sum̃ Total p⁹dict Recept⁹.

A° dm̃. p⁹dict.

Paymẽts by the seyd Edmñde ffletcher And Wyllm̃ Thompson, ɀc.,
ut seq̃.

In p⁹imis gyfne towards of yᵉ Repacon of Wyssyngsett⎫
Chyrche wᶜʰ pysshed thorow yᵉ ffall of y° pyñacle, ⎬ v*s.*
ɀc.     .     .     .     .     .     .     .     .⎭

Itm̃ to Wyllm̃ ffyncke for sowdyng of y° sowthe Eale⎫
of yᵉ Chyrche, ɀc., s. for his labour, com̃ons, ɀ ⎬ vj*s.*
Metall .     .     .     .     .     .     .⎭

Itm̃ to Herry Swanton s⁹uying hym then, that is to⎫
seye, for hys Com̃ons ɀ wags, the seyd tyme, ɀc. . ⎭ ij*s.*   xj*d.*

Itm̃ to Robt Clercke for his Com̃ons ɀ wags, dygyng⎫
down of yᵉ olde wall ⁽⁸²⁾ of y° northe syde of yᵉ ⎪
Chyrche wher y° new pales now stondyth, iij ⎬ xviij*d.*
dayes, ɀc.   ˎ     .     .     .     .     .⎭

Itm̃ to Wyllm̃ ffyncke ɀ ffather Heere for ther Com̃ons⎫
ɀ wags in mendyng of yᵉ Chyrche wall agey⁹st ⎬ xiij*d.*
ffra⁹cke .     .     .     .     .     .     .⎭

Itm̃ to Lamberd for mendyng of yᵉ Steple wyndowos ɀ⎫
makyng of yᵉ Chyrche Gat at yᵉ northe Style, ⎪
xiiij*d.* And vnto Ry. Purdye for hangells ɀ nayls ⎬ ij*s.*   ij*d.*
for y° sayd gate, xij*d.* .     .     .     .⎭

ñ. Itm̃ for oͬ Costes ᵹ s̃ᵖten other of yᵉ moste Awncyent
men of yᵉ Town Cõmanded to Aper ᵹ bryng An
Inuentarye of yᵉ Chyrche Goods [83] before yᵉ     vijs. iiijd.
Kynges Mayesties Cõmyssyoners at Walsynghm̃,
ᵹc. . . . . . . . . .

Itm̃ to Anderson for his Cõmons ᵹ wags in grauẏg of
fflaggs for yᵉ Chyrche walls, ijs. xd.; ᵹ to Thõms
Clercke ᵹ Herry ffyld for layeng of yᵉ sayd fflaggs,    iijs.   vjd.
viijd., ᵹc. . . . . . . . .

Sum̃, xxviijs. vjd. ᵹ xijd. ū. pᵍ (ut patet).

Itm̃ to A Mason xjᵗʰ dayes for mendyng of yᵉ Chyrche
walls, s. for his wags yᵉ sayd tyme, iiijs. vijd.; ᵹ
to Wyllm̃ ffraᵖckelyng for hys Cõmons the seyd   viijs.   xjd.
tyme, iiijs. iiijd. . . . . . . .

Itm̃ to Lyngey ᵹ Swanton for yᵉͬ Cõmons ᵹ wages in
sᵖuyng of hym the seyd tyme . . .     vs.   vjd.

Itm̃ to Wyllm̃ ffranckelyng for hys paynes ᵹ Costs in
Rydyng to Walsynghm̃ of yᵉ Townes busynes
when we wer Coᵖmāded to Aper befor yᵉ seyd      iiijd.
Commyssyoners . . . . . . .

Itm̃ to Wyllm̃ Purdy for palyng of pte of the Chyrche
yard, s. of yᵉ northe syde yᵉͬof, viijs. iiijd. And   ixs.   vjd.
for nayles for yᵉ seyde pales, ᵹc., xiiijd. . .

Itm̃ payed for yᵉ booke of yᵉ new sᵖuys [84] wᵗ yᵉ Costs
ᵹ Chargs of hym yᵗ bought yt, ᵹc. . . .   vjs.

Itm̃ to Wyllm Purdy for boords for yᵉ Mynystryng
Table, ijs.; ᵹ ffor Sooles for the sayd Table, xxjd.   iijs. ixd.

Itm̃ for breadd ᵹ wyne to Celebrate wᵗ bought at dyᵘse
tymes for yᵉ Communycants yer, ᵹc. . . .   vs.   vjd.

G 2

Itm̃ to Ḣerry ffylde for makyng of A dytche vnder yᵉ ⎫
Chyrche wall, s. At yᵉ Easte Style yᵉʳ, ₵c. . .⎭    xij*d.*

      Sum̃, xxxviij*s.* vj*d.* ₵ ij*s.* ū p⁹ (ut patet.)

Itm̃ to a Smẏthe for new Alteryng ₵ trymyng of yᵉ ⎫
Clocke, vij*s.*; To Rychard ffrauckelyng for his ⎬ ix*s.*   ix*d.*
Comons, ij*s.*; ₵ ffor wyer for the seyd Clocke, ix*d.* ⎭

Itm̃ payed to yᵉ Constables of Gressenhale for the Taxe ⎫
of yᵉ Town lands of Elmhm̃, iiij*d.* And to yᵒ Con- ⎬ v*s.*   iiij*d.*
tables of Betele for yᵉ Taxe of yᵉ sayd landes, v*s.* .⎭

Itm̃ to Thom̃s Shetell for carryeng of fflaggs for yᵉ ⎫
couyng of yᵉ Chyrche walls aforseyd, ₵c. . .⎭    xvj*d.*

Itm̃ to Roḃt Bartrhm̃ for mendyng yᵉ gret bell ⎫
wheale . . . . . . . . ⎬ [no entry.]

Itm̃ to Thom̃s Wakefelde for a hok for a ffalgate . .    ij*d.*

Itm̃ to yᵉ Balye of yᵉ mañ for yᵉ Rente of the Town ⎫
lands of Elmhm̃ lyeng wᵗin Betele . . .⎭    v*s.*

Redd*ᵗ* sol⁹. Itm̃ to yᵉ Colour of yᵉ lord of yᵉ sayd mañ for the ⎫
Rente of yᵉ sayd lands lyeng wᵗin Elmhm̃, ₵c. .⎭    vij*s.*

Itm̃ for yᵉ leate ffee for yᵉ seyd Townchype, ₵c. . . xxiiij*s.*

Itm̃ to my Lady Hastyngs Balye for yᵉ Rente of the ⎫
sayd lands, vj*d.*; ₵ for Rent payed to yᵉ Chapell of ⎬ vj*s.*   vj*d.*
Becke, vj*s.* . . . . . . . .⎭

Itm̃ to Thom̃s Wakefelde for a hooke, A verdwell, And ⎫
for yron for yᵉ gret Bell wheale, ₵c. . . .⎭    v*d.* oḃ

Itm̃ for oʳ Costs ₵ other Comanded to bryng yᵉ Chyrche ⎫
Goods wᵗ yᵉʳ Inue⁹tarye of yᵉ same,⁽⁸⁵⁾ Bells ₵ a ⎪
payer of chalyce onlye excepted, before yᵉ Kyngs ⎬ vj*s.*
Mayesties Co⁹myssioners at Lenne yᵉ xiijᵗʰ day of ⎪
June, in yᵉ vijᵗʰ yere of hys gracs Reygn, ₵c. .⎭

         Sum̃, iij*li.* v*s.* vj*d.* oḃ.

The wholl suñe of yᵉ Reč of yᵉ seyd Edmñde
ffletcher And Wyllñ Tompson ffor the yere } vj*li*. xix*s*. ij*d*.
Aforseyd, ys. . . . . . . .
The whole suñe of ther Chargs yᵉ sayd yere, ys . vj*li*. xv*s*. vj*d*. ob
And so remayn in yᵉʳ hands as ys heare layde }
down at ther Accompts All thyngs dyscharged } ‧iij*s*. vij*d*. ob
And dewe then to be rekened and payed, &c. } ut seq̃
And so the seyd Edmñde ffletcher & Wyllñ Thompson & yᵉʳ
heyres be clerly dyscharged for thys yere paste. Et sic quieti
sñt Anno pᵈdicto.

A° Dm.                              A° dñ, 1556.[86]

1556.     Mᵈ. A Rekenyng made vpon Trynytie Sondaye, the yere of oʳ Lorde
1° 4° Ph.   god M cccc lvj of Nycholas Purdy & Wᵐ Rudde, Chyrche-
: Mary.]    wardens, the yere be fore the deate hereof, of all ther Recᵗˢ &
wo years,   Paymẽts, as here aftʳ folueth.
. 1554 &   In pᵒms delyuᵒed to yᵉᵐ at ther Accõpts the yere of oʳ }
155, are      Lorde god M cccc lv . . . . . . . } xxx*s*.
ire passed  Itñ Reč by them for londeferme inpᵒms of Thomas }
er in the
ccounts.    Marche, xiij*s*. iiij*d*. ; of Rychard Crowe, }
            iij*s*. iiij*d*. ; Robart Rudde, x*s*. ; Wᵐ sõme, }
            ij*s*. viij*d*.; Symone Shetyll for the towe closse & }
            londs in the felde, xxi*s*. viij*d*.; Thomas Lussher for }
            the Capȳge Closse, iij*s*. iiij*d*. ; Wᵐ Thomson, }
            xij*d*.; Wᵐ Rudde, x*d*.; Edward hanforthe, x*d*.; } Sñ.
            Thomas Powle, xij*d*.; Rychard Ruston, xij*d*.; } iij*li*. ix*s*.ij*d*.
            Nycholas Purdy, x*d*.; Wᵐ franckelynge, xiij*d*.; Wᵐ }
            Bacche, xij*d*.; Wᵐ Egrym, viij*d*.; Thomas Clarke, }
            vj*d*.; John Johnsñ, xij*d*.; Wᵐ Smythe, iiij*d*.; }
            Harry Ruston, ij*s*.; Harry ffylde, ix*d*.; John }
            Broue mers², xij*d*.; Rychard Pycher, x*d*.; John }
            Garret, ij*d*. . . . . . . . . }

            Sñ tota², iiij*li*. xix*s*. ij*d*. Whareof

Inp⁹imis pᵈ to thomas Powle for wasshynge of the
Chyrche Clothes, xijd.; to John Browͤe for wrytynge
of a booke, ijd.; To the Pluñer for Sowde ᵹ lede,
vs. xd.; To dyxe for his borde, thre dayes, xvd.;
Wᵐ Browͤe for sᵖuynge the Ploñer, xxjd.; To hoñe
for wrytynge the Renttall in parchmͤt, ijd.; Itñ
pᵈ for wrytynge of the taske⁽⁸⁷⁾ booke, iiijd.; To
fyncke for settynge in the pully oͩ the founͬte,
viijd.; To harry Ruston for the pece of tymbe⁹, jd.;
for the Chyrchereues ᵹ the queste menes⁽⁸⁸⁾ Costs
whan they wer before the Vysetors at Walssyng-
hñe, xxd.; for mendynge of the Voyle, vjd.; payde
for A lyne for the funte, iijd.; To Annys
gryme ᵹ to a pore Woman, vd.; to the bell foͩder,
xixd.; To Robart Clarke for gatherynge ᵹ Caryenge
of Stone in to the hey waye, xxd.; pᵈ for the
quest mͤs Costes at Lychehñ, xxd.; to Symon
Shytyll ᵹ Thomas Lussher for ther Cost at
Lychehñ whan they wer quest men, xd.; for
ellmhñ taske, vjs. iiijd.; pᵈ for beteley taske, vs.;
gressnall, ijd.; pᵈ to Wᵐ Rudde for fecheynge of
a booke from foxley, ijd.; pᵈ for leyt ffee, xxiiijs.;
pᵈ for beteley Rent, vs.; pᵈ for the Rent of the

redd solut⁹.    Chappell of becke, vjs.; pᵈ for Ellmhñ Rent, vijs.;
pᵈ to hanfors Wyffe for mendynge of the Shyrplys,
iijd.; to John Broͩe mes⁹ for lynyng Clothe, ijd. oᵬ;
To Wᵐ Rudde for Carynge yᵉ englyshe books⁽⁸⁹⁾ to
Norwyche, vjd.; to Powle for wasshynge of the
Chyrche Clothes, xijd.

Paymͤts Sñ tota⁹, iijℓi. xvs. vd. oᵬ.

rthelmhm.
A° Dm.
57 to 1560.
6°Ph.&Mary
1° 2° 3° Eliz.]

A Reckeninge or Accompte made by Rychard ffrankelinge & Symon Shetyll, churchwardens ther, ye xvᵗʰ day of Aprell, Anno Regni Elizabeth, Anglie Regine Tercio (A.D. 1560), for five hole yeres then ended.

Arrerages. They receyued none.

Recepts. Rec̄ by them to th'use of yᵉ Towne, as it doth pticlerlye appere by ther Rentals.

Payments. Itm̄ paied by them as it doth pticlerly appere by ther bill of necessaryc charges redd and examyned.

Rychard ffranckelinge . xiijd.

So ther is in sᵒrplusage to them . . . . xxxs. iijd.

orthelmhm.
° Dm. 1561.
A° 4° Eliz.]

A Remembruñs of an accompte to be made (by) Wyllm̄ Batche, one of the Chyrche Wardens of the towne aforeseid, of & vppon all londs fearmeȝ and other suñes of money by hym from the feast of Pentycost A° iijᵗⁱᵒ dñe Regine nūc vntyll the last daye of maye A° iiijᵒ (1561) dñe Regine pᵒdce.

Inpᵒmis the seid Willm̄ dothe charge hym selff to have rec̄ of Thom̄s ffrankelyn for londe fearme } xijd.

Itm̄ of John Pereȝ for londe fearme . . xd.

Itm̄ of Edward hanford . . xd.

Itm̄ of John Pereȝ . . . vjd.

Itm̄ of Thom̄s ffrankelyn . vjd.

Itm̄ of Stephen Purdy . . xd.

Itm̄ of Symond Blomefeyld . xijd.

Itm̄ of Rob̄t Lussher . viijd.

Itm̄ of Stephen Purdye . . vjd.

Itm̄ of Wyllm̄ Smythe iiijd.

Itm̄ of Rychard Purdy . xviijd.

Itm̃ of Roḃt Barshm̃ .    . . . .  vjd.
Itm̃ of Willm̃ Skypper    . . . . xiijs. iiijd.

         Sum̃, xxijs. iiijd.


Itm̃ of Symon Shyttill. .  . . . . ijs. viijd.
Itm̃ of Roḃt Lussher . .  . . . . ixd.
Itm̃ of James Taverner [90] .  . . .  xijd.
Itm̃ of John Browne . .  . . .  xxijd.
Itm̃ of Roḃt Rudde . .  . . .  xs.
Itm̃ of Wyllm̃ Batche.  . . . . iijs. iiijd.
Itm̃ of Thom̃s Some .  . . . ijs. viijd.
Itm̃ of Rychard Crowe  . . . . iijs. iiijd.

        Sm̃, xxvs. vijd.
       Sm̃ totĩs, xlvijs. xjd.

| | |
|---|---|
| Itm̃ reč for a towne Close ly-inge in be-telye, then occupied by Simon Shittell then Churche Warden, xxs. | Itm̃ the seid accomptant dothe further Charge hym selff with xls. by hym reč of Henry Heyward for the Income of a leasse by hym latelie taken of & by the consent of the hole towneshipp aforeseid of the towne Clos lyeng in Beteley to hym leaton for the t^{9}me of x yeres . . . . .   xls. |

       Sm̃ totĩs reč, vli. vijs. xjd. wherof

  the seid Wyllm̃ dothe aske allowans as followethe, vz.—
In p^{o}imis layde out att Walsinghm̃ att the vysytacon . ijs. xjd. oḃ
Itm̃ for a Chalder of lyme . . . . . vs.

       Sm̃, vijs. xjd. oḃ


Itm̃ to Martons for vj lods of stone Caryeng from the tower [91] . . . . . . . .  viijd.

Itm̃ for dyggyng of the seid stone . . . . iiij*d.*

Itm̃ to iij masons for iiij daye₃ Works for their Wags ⎱ viijs. vij*d.*
& Bourde . . . . . . . ⎰

Itm̃ for nayles, j*d.*; a quarte of Wyne, vj*d.* . . . vij*d.*

Itm̃ to M<sup>r</sup> Coke for Councell (92) for makyng of our ⎱ xvijs. iiij*d.*
Wrytings . . . . . . . . ⎰

Itm̃ for Lete ffee . . . . . . . . xxiiijs.

Itm̃ to the Balyff of Elmehm̃ for rent due att Miche₃ ⎱ iijs. vj*d.*
last . . . . . . . . . ⎰

Itm̃ to the Baylyff of Beteley for rent due att the seid ⎱ ijs. vj*d.*
feast . . . . . . . . . ⎰

Itm̃ to M<sup>r</sup> Curson for rent then due for the hole yere . vjs.

Itm̃ for the sute ffyne of the londs in Beteley & Elmehm̃ iiij*d.*

Itm̃ for one Pottell of Wyne bought att Creistemas last xij*d.*

Itm̃ to the pson of Beteley for the Buttalls makyng of ⎱ iiij*d.*
our londs in Beteley . . . . . . ⎰

Sum̃, lxvs. ij*d.*

Itm̃ for our Chargs att the Chapettle Court att Lytchm̃ xij*d.*

Itm̃ to Thom̃s Stefenson for the Kepyn of ffylds sonn ⎱ xxs.
by the agrement of the towne . . . . ⎰

Itm̃ to Henry Wakefeyld for takyng downe of the rode ⎱ iijs. ij*d.*
lofte (93) . . . . . . . . ⎰

Itm̃ to Henry Beu<sup>v</sup>ley for one daye₃ Worke . . viij*d.*

Itm̃ for the x Com̃andyments (94) . . . . xvj*d.*

Itm̃ for one Pottell of Wyne on Mandy thrysdaye . xij*d.*

Itm̃ for Breadd ageinst Ester . . . . vj*d.*

Itm̃ to the Pryours baylyff for rent . . . . ij*d.*

Itm̃ to the house of Carbroke for rent for iij yere₃ . vj*d.*

redd$^t$ solut̃. Itm̃ for the halff yere; rent of our londs in Beteley & ⎫
  Elmehm̃ due att o$^r$ Ladie laste   .   .   .   .⎭   vj$s$.

Itm̃ for the bysshopps iniounccions [95] .        .        xij$d$.

Itm̃ for a Pottell of Wyne .     .     .        .        xij$d$.

Sm̃, v$li$. ix$s$.                    Sm̃, xxxvj$s$. j$d$.
v$d$. ob̃.                         Sm̃ alloc̃$^9$, cix$s$. v$d$. ob̃ And so.


A$^o$ Dm.     Received bye me, Wyllm̃ Bache, churchewarden of the town of
1562.             northelmhm̃, these somes of monye here aft$^r$ folowinge—
[A$^o$5$^o$Eliz.]

                       Anno R. R$s$. E. v$^o$.

In p$^9$imis Received for Rents & fearmes     .        .     l$s$.  iiij$d$.

Itm̃ for the fearme of the town close  .     .     .     xxxiij$s$. iiij$d$.

        Laid oute to the vse of the town of northelmhm̃ aforesaid in the
              yeare aforesaid by me wyllm̃ bache as here foloweth—

In p$^9$mis for a pottell of malmesaye ageinste whitson-⎫
  daye   .    .    .    .    .    .    .    .⎭        xij$d$.

Itm̃ to John brown for Leate fee .   .    .         . xxiiij$s$.

Itm̃ for the town Londs in elmhm̃ & beteley.        .   vj$s$.

Itm̃ for the suite fyne of the town Londs [96]        .        iiij$d$.

Itm̃ to the p$^9$ours balye     .    .             .        j$d$.

Itm̃ to M$^r$ cursons balye    .    .    .    .        .  vj$s$.

Itm̃ to m$^r$ harward for ij yeares Rents .    .    .        xij$d$.

Itm̃ for a newe saulter [97]    .    .    .    .    .    .    xxij$d$.

Itm̃ to Wyllm̃ Laws one daye gravinge of flagges for⎫
  the churche walles    .    .    .    .    .⎭        vj$d$.

Itm̃ to Wyllm̃ Laws & And$^9$son one daye gravinge of⎫
  flaggs .    .    .    .    .    .    .    .⎭        xiiij$d$.

Itm̃ at the sperytuall courte at Lychm̃ the puttinge in⎫
  of the copies of the Regist$^r$ booke & other chargs .⎭  ij$s$.

Itm̃ for halfe a white Lether hide for the bell clappers .     ij$s$. iiij$d$.

Itm̄ for Layenge vp of the flaggs vpon the churche }
wall . . . . . . . . . } (illegible)
Itm̄ for wyne ageinste chrystemes . . . iijd.
Itm̄ one pinte of wyne ageinste cādlemes . . . iijd.
Itm̄ for halfe an hundred nailes and the makynge of }
the churche gate . . . . . . . } iiijd.
Itm̄ one gallon ⁊ a pinte of malmeseye ageinste Easter ijs. iijd.
reddᵗ solᵖ Itm̄ for the Rente of the town Londs of elmhm̄ ⁊ }
beteleye at the Annuncyacōn of oʳ Ladie . . } vjs.

Sm̄, lvs. vd.

Aº Dm.           Aº R. Rs. E. vjº.
1563.    Reꝯ in Rentes ⁊ Fearmes . . . . . ls. iiijd.
[Aº 6º   Itm̄ for the town close one halfe yeare . . . . xxxiijs. iiijd.
Eliz.]                    Sum̄a, iiijli. iijs. viijd.

Laid oute of the same as foloweth—
In pᵖmis to the plomᵖ ⁊ his manne, ⁊ for Sowde and }
nayles, ⁊ for wode . . . . . . } xijs. vjd.
Itm̄ for a pinte of wyne ageinste whitsondaye . . iijd.
Itm̄ at swaffhm̄ before the quiens collectoʳ for the town }
Londs . . . . . . . . . } iiijs. viijd.
Itm̄ at the spirituall courte at Lichm̄ . . xijd.
Itm̄ for the Leete fee . . . . . . xxiiijs.
Itm̄ for the town Londs in Elmhm̄ ⁊ beteleye vjs.
Itm̄ for the suite fyne . . iiijd.
Itm̄ to the pᵖoures balye jd.
Itm̄ to Mʳ cursons balye . vjs.
Itm̄ to Mʳ harward . . . . . . vjd.
Itm̄ for the taske of the town Londs in beteleye . vs.

Itm̃ to ij menne one daye fellynge ₰ Breakinge of tymber for pales for the Churcheyard . . } xiiij*d*.

Itm̃ for Carienge of the said tymber . . . . xx*d*.

Itm̃ to willm̃ fyncke for glasinge of the chappell wyndowe; for wode . . . . . . } xx*d*.

Itm̃ for a pinte of wyne ageinste hallowmes . . . iij*d*.

Itm̃ for the newe homelye booke[98] . . . . iiij*s*.

Itm̃ to beu⁹leye one daye mendinge the pavement in the churche . . . . . . . . } vj*d*.

Itm̃ to the plom̃ for one daies worke . . . . xij*d*.

Itm̃ for a pinte of wyne ageinst cãdlemes . . . iij*d*.

Itm̃ to willm̃ fincke for glasinge and mendinge the windows about the churche . . . . } xvj*s*.
Itm̃ for wode . . . . . . . . . }

Itm̃ one gallon ₰ a pottell of wyne ageinst East⁹ . iij*s*.

Itm̃ for breade for the com̃union . . . . . vj*d*.

Redd^t sol⁹. Itm̃ for the halfe yeares Rente of the town Londs in clmhm̃ ₰ beteleye . . . . . . } vj*s*.

Sm̃, iiij*li*. xvj*s*. iiij*d*.

A° Dm. 　　　　　　　A° R. Rs. E. vij°.
1564.　　Rec̃ for Rents ₰ fearmes . . . . l*s*. iiij*d*.
[A°7° Eliz.] ₰ for the towne close in Beateleye . xxxiij*s*. iiij*d*.

### Laid oute as foloweth—

In p̃imis a pinte of Wine ageinst hallowe thursdaye . iij*d*.

Itm̃ at swaffhm̃ before quiens collecto^r for the town Londs . . . . . . . . } xvj*d*.

Itm̃ to M^r yelvertons clerke for makinge of the pasporte for the child to go to Windhm̃ . } iiij*d*.

Itm̃ for nourcenge the same childe . . . . iij*s*. iiij*d*.

Itm̃ to thom̃s franckelin & Robt basbm̃ & m̃garete heare for carienge the said child to windhm̃ . . . } ijs. iiijd.

Itm̃ for the taske of the town Londs to gresnhall . ijd.

Itm̃ a pinte of wine ageinst m̃chelmes . . . . iiijd.

Itm̃ for the Leete fee of the town Londs . . . xxiiijs.

Itm̃ for the Rente of the town Londs in Elmhm̃ & beteleye . . . . . . . . } vjs.

Itm̃ for m̃cyment of the town Londs . . . . ixd.

Itm̃ to the p̃ours balye . . . . . . . jd.

Itm̃ to M^r cursons balye . . . . . . vjs.

Itm̃ to wyllm̃ fincke for xxxij^tl quarrells of glasse & seven pounds of Leadd & one pounde of sowde . } vjs.

Itm̃ for woode . . . . . . . .

Itm̃ to Edward hanforth for Ryvinge of pales . . xxd.

Itm̃ to ij menne one daye for palinge of the churche yard . . . . . . . . . } xvjd.

Itm̃ one gallon & a pottell of wyne agẽist cst^o . . iijs.

Redd^t Itm̃ for the Rente of the town Londs in Elmhm̃ & beteleye . . . . . . . } vjs.

Sm̃, iijli. ijs. xd.

**A° Dm.**        Anno R. Rs. E. viij°.

**1565.** Rec̃ in Rents & fearmes . . . . . ls. iiijd.

**A°8°Eliz.]** & for the towne close in Beetleye . . . xxxiijs. iiijd.

Laid oute as foloweth—

In p^omis to Ruston for a paier of shoes for cavstons Davghter . . . . . . . } vjd.

Itm̃ for com̃union breade . . . . . . iiijd.

Itm̃ at the spirytuall courte at Lychm̃ . . . . iiijd.

Itm̃ for wyne betwixte est & midsom̃ one quarte of wyne . vjd.

Itm̃ for ij hookes for the heith gate . . . .    **x**d.

Itm̃ for the Leete fee of the town Londs . . . **xxiiij**s.

Itm̃ for the Rente of the town Londs in Elmhm̃ &c &#125;   **vj**s.
beteleye . . . . . . .&#125;

Itm̃ for suite fyne . . . . . . .    **iiij**d.

Itm̃ to the p⁹ours balye . . . .    **j**d.

Itm̃ to M<sup>r</sup> cleares balye . . .   **vj**s.

Itm̃ to M<sup>r</sup> harward for ij yeares . .    **xij**d·

Itm̃ at the spirituall courte at Lychm̃ . . . .    **vj**d.

Itm̃ to willm̃ Laws for scourringe of a Dike at thorne- &#125;   **x**d.
well . . . . . . . . .&#125;

Itm̃ for nailes for the town stockes &c wedges for the bell &#125;   **ij**d.
gudgions . . . . . . .&#125;

Itm̃ for a pinte of wine ageinste cãdlemes . . .    **iiij**d.

Itm̃ for halfe a white Lether hide for the bell clappers   **ij**s.

Itm̃ to John Curtes one daye makinge the bell bawd- &#125;   **vij**d.
rickes . . . . . . . .&#125;

Itm̃ for thre pottells of malmesaye ageinst Easter . **iij**s.

Itm̃ for the Rente of the town Londs in Elmhm̃ &c &#125;   **vj**s.
beteleye . . . . . .&#125;

                   Sum̃, liij**s**. iij**d**.

---

**A° Dm.**                  Anno R. Rs. E. ix°.

**1566.**   Reĉ in Rents &c fearmes . . . . . **l**s. **iiij**d.

[A°9°Eliz.] &c for the towne close in Beetleye . . . . **xxxiij**s. **iiij**d.

              Laid oute as foloweth—

In p⁹mis to willm̃ walden for one daye gravinge of &#125;   **vij**d.
flaggs . . . . . . . . .&#125;

Itm̃ for the firste tome of homelies &c the quiens Iniunc- &#125;   **xvij**d.
tyons . . . . . . . .&#125;

Itm p$^d$ to m$^r$ ducket for comunyon bread & a boxe     .        xiiij$d$.

Itm for mendinge the clocke to m$^r$ ducket  .    .    .          x$d$.

Itm to the plom & hs manne for their wags & borde ⎱ v$s$.
thre daies  .    .    .    .    .    .    .    ⎰

Itm for iiij pounds sowde & halfe an hundred Leadd ⎱
nayles  .    .    .    .    .    .    .    .    ⎰ iij$s$.   x$d$.

Itm for woode  .    .    .    .    .    .    .

Itm to willm fyncke for xxxij$^{ti}$ quarrells of glasse    .    ij$s$.  viij$d$.

Itm for iiij pounds & an halfe of Leadd    .    .    .        xiij$d$.

Itm for halfe a pound of sowd & ij fote & an halfe of ⎱
uewe glasse  .    .    .    .    .    .    .    ⎰ xxij$d$.

Itm for woode  .    .    .    .    .    .    .

Itm a pinte of Wine ageinst mihelmes.    .    .    .          iij$d$.

Itm to John brown for the Leete fee    .    .    .    . xxiiij$s$.

Itm for the Rente of the town Londs in Elmhm & ⎱ vj$s$.
beteleye  .    .    .    .    .    .    .    ⎰

Itm for mcyamet of the butts    .    .    .    .    .    vj$s$.  viij$d$.

Itm for office Lond of the tente fost$^?$ [99]    .    .    .        vij$d$.

Itm to the p$^?$oures balye    .    .    .    .    .    .          j$d$.

Itm to m$^r$ straunges [100] balye for Rente & suite fyne    .        ix$d$.

Itm to m$^r$ cleares balye for Rente.    .    .    .    .    vj$s$.

Itm to s$^?$ John franckelin, clerke, [101] for mendinge ⎱ viij$d$.
billingforth Bridge    .    .    .    .    .    ⎰

Itm to thoms franckelin for the clarke of the mket for ⎱ iiij$d$.
ij yeares  .    .    .    .    .    .    .    ⎰

Itm for one pottell of malmeseye & iij qrts of Redd ⎱
wine ageinste est & comunion breade    .    .    ⎰ ij$s$.

Itm for the Rente of the town Londs in Elmhm & ⎱ vj$s$.
beteleye  .    .    .    .    .    .    .    ⎰

Itm to willm Laws & willm walden for mendinge ⎱
the Ryver at Kings mille    .    .    .    .    ⎰ xx$d$.

H

Itm̃ at the vysytacon for c̃ten bookes ʒ other chargs .    v*s*.

Itm̃ for a pinte of malmeseye ageinste whitsondaye⎫
Last    . . . . . . .⎭    iij*d*.

Itm̃ for puttinge in the copie of the Regisᵗ . . .    iiij*d*.

Sum̃, iij*li*. xix*s*. j*d*.

A° R. Rs. E. x°.

**A° Dm.**
**1567.**
**[A° 10°**
**Eliz.]**

Reč in Rents ʒ fearmes . . . . . . .    l*s*. iiij*d*.

ʒ for the towne close in Beeteleye . . . . xxxij*s*. iij*d*.

Laid oute as folowethe—

Itm̃ to John Brown for the Lete fee . . . . xxiiij*s*.

Itm̃ to him for the Rente of the town Lond in Elmh̃m   iij*s*. vj*d*.

Itm̃ to Mʳ goggeneye (102) for the Rente of town Lond⎫
in beteley . . . . . . . .⎭    ij*s*. vj*d*.

Itm̃ to Mʳ cleres balye (103) for Rente . . . . vj*s*.

Itm̃ for the halfe taske of the towne Londs in beteleye⎫
ʒ gresnalle . . . . . . . .⎭    ij*s*. ij*d*.

Itm̃ to the pᵒours balye . . . . . .    j*d*.

Itm̃ to the plom̃ for a pounde of sowde ʒ a dayes worke⎫
aboute the churche Leads . . . . .⎭    xvj*d*.

Itm̃ for his borde . . . . . . . .    iiij*d*.

Itm̃ for a pinte of malmeseye ageynste christemes .    iij*d*.

Itm̃ for the communyon cuppe . . . . . xxxix*s*. viij*d*.

Itm̃ for iij pottells of Wyne ageinste easter ʒ for⎫
com̃unyon breade . . . . . .⎭    iij*s*. ij*d*.

Itm̃ for the Rente of the town Londs in elmh̃m ʒ⎫
beteleye . . . . . . . .⎭    vj*s*.

Itm̃ for the puttinge in of the copie of the Regisᵗ at⎫
easᵗ . . . . . . . . .⎭    iiij*d*.

Sum̃, iiij*li*. ix*s*. iiij*d*.

A° Dm.                A° R. Rs. E. xj°.

| | | |
|---|---|---|
| **1568.** | Reč in Rents ҁ fermes . . . . . . | ls. iiijd. |
| **l° 11°** | Itm̃ for the towne close . . . . | . xxxiijs. iiijd. |
| **Eliz.]** | | |

Laid oute as followeth—

| | |
|---|---|
| Inp<sup>9</sup>mis for the Lete fee . . . . . . | . xxiiijs. |
| Itm̃ for tho Rent of the town Lond in elmhm̃ . . | iijs. vjd. |
| Itm̃ for the Rente of the town Lond in beteleye . . | ijs. vjd. |
| Itm̃ to m<sup>r</sup> cleres balye for Rente . . . . . | vjs. |
| Itm̃ for the halfe taske of town Londs in beteleye ҁ gresnall . . . . . . . | ijs. ijd. |
| Itm̃ for an̂lcimēt of the butts . . . . . | iijd. |
| Itm̃ for a pinte of malmeseye ageinste mihelmes . . | iijd. |
| Itm̃ for mendinge of the porche dore . . . . | iijd. |
| Itm̃ to the smyth for mendinge of the Locke of the north Dore of the church . . . . . | iiijd. |
| Itm̃ for a pinte of Malmesaye ageinste christmas . . | iijd. |
| Itm̃ for three pottclls ageinste eas?̃ ҁ breade . . | iijs. ijd. |
| Itm̃ to m<sup>r</sup> sturges for vij yeares Rente of one Acre of Lond in m<sup>r</sup> tavern̂s close (104) . . . | xiiijd. |

Sum̃a, xliijs. xd.

| | | |
|---|---|---|
| **A° Dm.** | Vppon thacompte taken of Wylyam Batche for viij years, vꝫ from | |
| **1560 to** | a° iij° R. El., ҁc., vntill the feaste of pentecoste a° xj° w<sup>ch</sup> was | |
| **1568.** | taken the ix<sup>th</sup> of Marche a° xiiij°, yt appeereth— | |
| **A° 3°to 11°** | Bye thaccompte finished a° iiij° was dewe vnto him . | xviijd. ob |
| **Eliz.]** | Bye the accompte finished a° v° he oweth . . | . xxviijs. iijd. |
| | Bye the accompte finished a° vj° was dewe vnto him . | xijs. viijd. |
| | Bye the accompte finished a° vij° he oweth . . . | xxs. xd. |
| | Bye the accompte finished a° viij° he owethe . . | . xxxs. vd. |

Bye the accompte fynished a° ix° he owethe . . . iiijs̄. viijd.

Bye the accompte fynished a° x° was dewe vnto him . vs. viijd.

Bye the accompte fynished a° xj° he owethe . . . xxxiiis. xd

& so the receiptes be more then the disbursinges bye . vli. iiijs. ob

And after was alowed vnto the seyed accomptant
    bye the consent of the towne for certeyne
    moneye disbursed bye him to the behoufe   }   iijli. xvs. iiijd.
    of the seyed towne . . . . .

Itm̄ for a pottell of wine . . . . . . . xijd.

Itm̄ for a calender to the service booke (⸌) . . . iiijd.

Sic in toto, iiijli. xvjs. viijd.

W<sup>ch</sup> beinge abated owt of hys charge above wrytten }
    computatis computandis ther ys dewe to the towne } vijs. iiijd. ob

Thaccompte of Simon Shytle from the feaste of Pentecoste a° xj° R. Elizabethe vntill the ix<sup>th</sup> of Marche a° xiiij° eiusdem ioynctlye taken becawse he wolde not shewe the particular disbursinges of eche yere, duringe w<sup>ch</sup> iij yeres yt apperethe he charged him selfe onlye w<sup>t</sup> the receyptes as Batche had donne the other viij yeres.

Inprimis the seyed Simon Shytle ys charged for
    the rentes of one hole yere dewe at the feaste
    of S<sup>t</sup> Michaell the archangell a° xj° R.   }
    beside the towne close as in the former   } iiijli. iijs. viijd.
    accomptes w<sup>t</sup> ls. iiijd., & for the towne close
    xxxiijs. iiijd., sic in toto . . . . .

Itm̄ the seyed Simon ys lykewyse charged for one }
    other hole yeres rente dewe at the feaste of } iiijli. iijs. viijd.
    S<sup>t</sup> Michaell a° xij° . . . . . }

Itm̃ the seyed Simon ys lykewyse charged for one ⎫
other hole yeres rente dewe at the feaste ⎬ iiij*li.* iij*s.* viij*d.*
of S<sup>t</sup> Michaell a° xiij°, as in former accomptes ⎭

Itm̃ of the seyed Simon for ij mylche kye given to ⎫
the towne bye one Henrye Ruston, clerke   .   . ⎭ liij*s.* iiij*d.*

Itm̃ he ys lykewyse charged w<sup>t</sup> the rent of the seyed ⎫
kye for v yeres ended at the purification of owr ⎬ xxx*s.*
ladye laste paste at vj*s.* bye the yere   .   .   . ⎭

Itm̃ he ys lykewyse charged w<sup>t</sup> beinge gyven to the ⎫
towne bye the seyed Henrye Ruston   .   .   . ⎭ xx*s.*

Sum̃a omniũ re receptorum, xvij*li.* xiiij*s.* iiij*d.*


Unde petit allocari pvt sequitur—

Inprimis dewe vnto him vppon hys laste accompte ⎫
made a° iij° R. as   .   .   .   .   .   .   . ⎬ xxx*s.* iij*d.*

Itm̃ for breade ⁊ wine for com̃unicantes at Easter a° ⎫
xij° R.   .   .   .   .   .   .   .   .   . ⎬ iij*s.* ij*d.*

Itm̃ for breade ⁊ wine for com̃unicantes a° xiij°   .   . ij*s.* j*d.*

Itm̃ more for wine   .   .   .   .   .   .   . iij*d.*

Itm̃ for ij foxes heades accordinge to the statwte [106]   . ij*s.*

Itm̃ for iiij polecattes ⁊ a wilde cattes hed   .   .   . v*d.*

Itm̃ for the Leete fee dewe vnto the Lorde at the feaste ⎫
of S<sup>t</sup> Michaell, a° xj°   .   .   .   .   . ⎬ xxiiij*s.*

Itm̃ for the Leete fee dewe vnto the Lorde at the feaste ⎫
of S<sup>t</sup> Michaell, a° xij°   .   .   .   .   . ⎬ xxiiij*s.*

Itm̃ for the rente of the towne landes dewe vnto mye ⎫
L. for ij yeres ⁊ a halfe ended at the annunciation ⎬ xxx*s.*
of owr Ladye, a° xiij°   .   .   .   .   . ⎭

Itm̃ gyven to ij poore men   .   .   .   .   . x*d.*

Itm̃ given to a poore woman   .   .   .   . vj*d.*

Itm̃ for line for the towne net [107]    .    .    .    .    xiiij*d.*

Itm̃ for timber for peinforde bridge, & given to Edwarde ⎫
    Purdewe for a deyes work in mendinge the same . ⎭ iiij*s.*

Itm̃ for hys owne horse & carte & labor abowte the same    xij*d.*

Itm̃ at the generall at Licham    .    .    .    .    .    xij*d.*

Itm̃ for the amercyament of the towne neate    .    .    iijs.  iiij*d.*

Itm̃ for a bwll hide    .    .    .    .    .    ijs.  iiij*d.*

Itm̃ leyed owt for office lande    .    .    .    .    xiiij*d.*

Itm̃ to Springer for mendinge the Sawnce bell [108]    .    ijs.

Itm̃ for lime & cariadge of the same    .    .    .    xij*d.*

Itm̃ for a barre for a glasse windowe    .    .    .    iiij*d.*

Itm̃ for the taske of Beetleye    .    .    .    .    iiij*d.*

Itm̃ for the subsedye of the towne lande    .    .    iiijs.

Itm̃ for the dreyne skowringe at Thornwell .    .    .    iiij*d.*

Itm̃ at Hewghe Dikes bridall for wine .    .    .    j*d.*

Itm̃ at Richarde Reades bridall for wine    .    .    j*d.*

Itm̃ for the rente of the towne landes lying in Beeteleye ⎫
    dewe at the feaste of Sᵗ Michaell, xiij° R. E.    .⎭ ijs.  vj*d.*

Itm̃ for breade & wine for comũunicantes    .    .    vij*d.*

Itm̃ for the subsydye for the towne landes .    .    .    iiijs.

Itm̃ for bawdrickes for the bells .    .    .    .    xviij*d.*

Itm̃ peyed to wylyam finke for glasinge    .    .    .    xxs.

Itm̃ for a rooke net    .    .    .    .    .    ijs.  viij*d.*

Itm̃ at the chapitell    .    .    .    .    .    ijs.

Itm̃ at the makinge of the buttes    .    .    .    xij*d.*

Itm̃ peyed to wakefielde for a bar of yron .    .    .    x*d.*

Itm̃ for a pynte of wine    .    .    .    .    ij*d.*

Itm̃ for beekon watche.    .    .    .    iiijs.

Itm̃ to fletcher beinge gyven to Shypmen    .    .    xviij*d.*

                    Sum̃a, ix*li.* v*d.*

Et sic computatis computandis he owethe thys ⎰ viij*li*. xiij*s*. xj*d*.
ix^{th} of Marche to the towne . . . ⎱

And wiliam Batches det as befor appeerethe . . vij*s*. iiij*d*. oᵬ

Sic in toto, ix*li*. xv*d*. oᵬ.

A° Dm. | Thaccompt of John Fletcher, one of the churchewardens there, from
'71 to 1577 | the ix^{th} of m°che A° xiiij° Eliza., At w^{ch} tyme Symon Shittle
North- | left that office, vnto the vj^{th} of Aᵽll, Anno xix° eiusdm̃ Regīe,
mhm̃. | 1577, vℨ for v yerres and one monethe as folowethe—
ι° 14° to 19° | Inᵽmis he is to be Charged w^{th} the reᴄ̃ of the⎱
Eliz.] | Rentes of the towne land there for the said⎫
five yeres at iiij*li*. iij*s*. xj*d*. p An., payable at ⎬ xx*li*. 17*s*. 6*d*.
the feast of S^t Michaell tharca^9gell . . ⎭

So he ys to be Charged w^{th} the Arrerages of⎫
Symon Shittle, his Accompt beyng viij*li*. ⎬ ix*li*. xv*d*. oᵬ
xiij*s*. xj*d*., ⅋ for tharrerages of W^m batche⎪
p Cõsiti, vij*s*. iiij*d*. oᵬ. . . . ⎭

Also he ys to be Charged w^{th} xl*s*. pcell of a legacye of⎰ xl*s*.
iij*li*. geven to the towne by Henrie ruston, Clerk . ⎱

Sm̃, xxxj*li*. 18*s*. 9*d*. oᵬ.

Note.—This Account is crossed through, and at the end is written,
" Oñat^r in libr^9 novo."

A° Dm. N° ᵽ.
1549. A note of y^e laten (letting) of all suche pcell of londs beyng ffreholde
⅋ belongyng to y^e Townshype of northelmhm̃, Sytuate,
lyeng ⅋ beyng w'in y^e bownds of y^e fuylds of northelmhm̃
aforseyd, and of late wer in y^e occupyeng of wyllm̃ ffra^9ckelyng,
wyllm Lussher, Nycholas purdy, And Thom̃s Shetell. As by

A payer of Indentures between the Inhabytañce of yᵉ seyd Townchyppe ⁊ yᵉᵐ, beryng date yᵉ xxxiᵗⁱ yere of yᵉ reygn of oʳ late souᵖayn Lord Kyng Henry the viijᵗʰ, more playnly dothe Apere, wᵗ other pcells also ptaynyng to yᵉ seyd Townchyppe, beyng Copyholde. As here Aftᵖ benethe in ther seuᵖall pcells more playnly shall Apere. And vnto whom they be now laten, And in what ptes of yᵉ ffuylds they lye, wrytten yᵉ iiijᵗʰ daye of Nouember, the yere of oʳ Lord Mˡˡccccc ⁊ xlixᵗⁱ, And in yᵉ iiijᵗʰ yere of yᵉ Reygne of oʳ most souᵖayn Lord Kyng Edward yᵉ syxt that now ys, ⁊c., And wer laten by the Chyrchwardens yᵉʳ, that is to seye, Wyllm̃ ffraᵖckelyng ⁊ Herry Ruston, wᵗ yᵉ Assent ⁊ consent of yᵉ resydue of yᵉ Inhabytañce yᵉʳ, froᵖ yᵉ ffest of Seynt Mychaell the Archaᵖgell laste paste next befor yᵉ date herof, for one wholl yere, And so froᵖ yere to yere aftᵖ yᵗ, by the space of teen yers in all, To these onely entents ⁊ purposes, that is to seye, After yᵉ Rents ⁊ other Chargs to yᵉ seyd londs Apptaynyng beyng payed ⁊ dyscharged, The rest to be payed towards yᵉ paymēt of the Taxe or fysten of oʳ seyd souᵖayn yᵉ Kyng ⁊ of hys Successours from tyme to tyme, beyng Kyngs of yˡˢ Realme, As often as Any suche Taxe or ffyfteᵖ heraftrᵖ shalbe taxed, Charged, demāded, or leuyed wᵗin or vpon yᵉ seyd Inhabytañce or Townchyppe froᵖ tyme to tyme. And euᵖy of yᵉᵐ to whom yᵉ seyd londs be now laten, whose names heraftrᵖ folowethe, shall yerlye paye for euᵖy pcell they haue suche Som̃es of monye As herafter shall be mencyoned to yᵉ seyd Wyllm̃ ffraᵖckelyng ⁊ Herry Rustñ, now beyng Chyrchwardens, ⁊ to yᵉʳ Successours froᵖ tyme to tyme beyng, duryng ther seyd Lease, ⁊c.

Vritten in ñargin in iifferent :riting, "now ʰoũs franklyng."

Lib. { In p̃imis to Wyllm̃ Thompson, 1 Acrᵖ lyeng at Spylcoks  
Townesende  .    .    .    .    .    .    .    . } xijd.

Lib. { Itm̃ to Symon Shetell, j Acr⁹ lyeng in same ffyrlonge } xijd.
       { ther . . . . . . . . . } ɛviijd.

Lib. Itm̃ to Wyllm̃ Rudd j Acr⁹ lyeng at Syluerdeane . xd.

Lib. Itm̃ to Edward Handeforthe j Acr⁹ lyeing at Parckegate xd.

Lib. { Itm̃ to Thom̃as Powell too (sic) halfe Acr⁹ yᵉ one }
     { lyeng at Stretebusshes ɛ yᵉ other at Brods- } xijd.
     { lothe . . . . . . . . . }

Lib. { Itm̃ to Herry Swanton now Rychard Rustñs j half }
     { Acr⁹ lyeng at Blackhurnfyrlonge . . . . } iiijd.

Lib. { Itm̃ to the seyd Rychard Rustñ j Acr' lyeng in the }
     { same ffy ʳlonge . . . . . . } viijd.

Lib. { Itm̃ to Nycholas Purdye j Acr⁹ lyeng at the west end }
     { of Blomefelds closse . . . . . } xd.

Lib. { Itm̃ to Wyllm̃ Yarrhm̃ j Acr⁹ lyeng in Blackhurfyrlong }
     { between yᵉ lands late of Sy. dethyk, genᵗ, ɛ Ry. } viijd.
     { Hey. (Heyward) yᵉ elder . . . . . }

Lib. { Itm̃ to Wyllm̃ ffranckelyng j Acr⁹ ɛ j Rode lyeng at }
     { Wells Townsende . . . . . . } xiijd.

Lib. { Itm̃ to Thom̃s Shetell j Acr⁹ ɛ j rode lyeng in poke- }
     { hyrne . . . . . . . . } xijd.

Lib. { Itm̃ to Wyllm̃ Egrym j Acr⁹ lyeng in Couerle- }
     { creste . . . . . . . } viijd.

Lib. { Itm̃ to Thom̃s Clercke j Acr⁹ lyeng in Edgegraue }
     { ffyrlong . . . . . . . } vjd.

Lib. { Itm̃ to John Johnson j Acr⁹ ɛ A halfe lyeng in hys }
     { Closse at the heathe . . . . . } xijd.

Lib. { Itm̃ to Wyllm̃ Smythe halff An Acr⁹ lyeng by }
     { Wodcoks Closse to yᵉ bromward . . . } iiijd.

Lib.
Nat⁹.
{ Itm̃ to Herry Rustñ ij Acr⁹, yᵉ one ffre, lieng at Holgate, ҁ one d. Acr⁹ fre lyeng also yᵉʳ, ҁ yᵉ other bond lyeng in Pelletts ffyrlong . . . } ijs.

Nat⁹.
{ Itm̃ to Herry ffylde j Acr⁹ ҁ An halfe lyeng in Paynots deale . . . . . . . } ixd.

Nat⁹.
{ Itm̃ to John Brown meas' j Acr⁹ lyeng in Pellets ffyrlong nygh leen waye . . . . . } xijd.

Nat⁹.
{ Itm̃ to Rychard Pytcher j Acr⁹ ҁ An halffe lyeng in Catberd ffyrlong . . . . . . . } xd.

ñ p⁹.
In w'nes of all ҁ syguler yᵉ p⁹myss; to be well ҁ ffaythfullye Accomplysshed and pformed on bothe yᵉ ptes aforseyd, These men folowyng be w'nesses to yᵉ same, that is to seye, s⁹ John Pecke,(109) clercke, John Elu⁹yche,(110) prest, John Pers, Wyllm̃ Purdy, wᵗ diu⁹se other of yᵉ Inhabytañce beyng ther ҁ then p⁹sent, ҁc.

At the foot of the last page of the Accounts is written, in a different handwriting :—

Itm̃ to Rycharde Blomfelde by the Chyrchewardens ҁ ye inhabitañce of elmham j acr⁹ and j rode lyeing in parkehyrne,
xijs. iiijd.

At the foot of the last page of the book is written :—

eche of ye⁹ received xxxvjs.

Willm̃ Rudd
Wᵐ Purdy } xxiijs.    Of yᵉ plowllett (111) .      xvjs.    xd.

Wᵐ Purdy
Willm̃ Tompsone }

# NOTES.

A° Dm.
1539.
(1) "Corpis X' gyld." Mr. Carthew, in the *Hundred of Launditch*, mentions four Guilds as existing in ancient times in North Elmham, viz.:—Gilda S. Mariæ, S. Johis, S. Jacobi, and Corpus Christi. The Parish Church is dedicated to S. Mary, and of the two chapels, the one on the south side of the choir to S. James, and the other on the north side to S. John. The ancient Guilds were friendly Trade Societies, to which each member paid a certain fee, called a guild, from the Saxon *gildan* (to pay).—See Brewer's *Phrase and Fable*, and Ashley's *Introduction to English Economic History and Theory*.

(2) "Lond ferme." Stephens defines ferme or feorme thus:—
"*Farm* or *feorme* is an old Saxon word signifying provisions, and it came to be used instead of *rent* or *render*, because anciently the greater part of rents were reserved in provisions—in corn, in poultry, and the like—till the use of money became more frequent; so that a farmer (*firmarius*) was one who held his lands upon payment of a rent or *feorme;* though at present, by a gradual departure from the original sense, the word *farm* is brought to signify the very estate or lands as held upon farm or rent."—See *Notes and Queries*, Long Perne Court, 7th S., vii. 109, Mar. 2, 1889.

(3)  "Hallowmes."   Hallowmas, the Mass or Feast of Allhallows,
*i.e.*, All Saints.   Shakespeare alludes to a custom on this day
(in *Two Gentlemen of Verona*, ii. 1, "to speak puling, like a
beggar at Hallowmas"; also *Richard II.*, v. 1), some traces of
which exist in Staffordshire, where the poor go from parish to
parish "a souling," *i.e.*, begging, in lamentable tones, for a kind of
cake called "soul cake," and singing a song called the "souler's
song."   The custom originally meant that the beggars should
pray for the souls of the giver's departed friends on the following
day, November 2nd, which was the Feast of All Souls.—*Nares'
Glossary*, 1859.   The constant reference to this festival in the
Churchwardens' Accounts would seem to indicate that it was
observed in the parish as a time of much feasting.   Funds appear
to have been collected for it, and any money over was paid to "y⁰
Towne stok."   No doubt a merry-making was combined with a
religious service.   It was an ancient custom, at this season, for the
guild brethren and sisters to assemble in church to pray that the
souls of the faithful departed, through the mercy of God, might
rest in peace.   Upon these occasions the guild priest or chaplain
used to read out from the pulpit the names of the departed, and say,
"Of your devout charity ye shall pray for all the brethren and
sisters of" such a guild in such a church.—See Carthew's *Hundred
of Launditch*, vol. ii., p. 593.

(4)  "John Taüner" (Taverner), the son of Nicholas Taverner of
North Elmham.   He died in 1545, at the age of 88, and was
buried at Brisley, leaving a widow, Anne, daughter of . . . . .
Crowe, of East Bilney, who followed him to the grave in or before
1557.   She was his second wife, the first having been Alice,
daughter of Robert Silvester of Brisley, who was, no doubt, related
to Richard Silvester, Vicar of Elmham from 1523 to 1541.   One
of John Taverner's sons was James, so well known in Elmham

annals for his hostility to the Crumwells. Another son was Richard, the author of Taverner's Bible. The Taverners were an ancient family, and arc said to have traced their descent from Ralf le Taverner, who held lands in Elmham in 1272, and Waryn his son in 1300. William, Waryn's youngest son, was of Dunwich in Suffolk, the ancient East Anglian see, and had a corrody or maintenance in the Abbey of Sibton in the 10th of Edward II. Sir Nicholas, the eldest, lived at Elmham. His son John le Taverner married Cecilia, daughter of one Gelham; and their son John distinguished himself at the battle of Agincourt. Henry, his elder brother, was a councillor-at-law, and held lands at Elmham at the time of his death in the 6th of Edward IV. ·

(5) "Cāpyng close." The Camping Close consisted of two acres of land to the east of the Church, where a game of ball, somewhat the same, I imagine, as our modern football, and called "camping," was played. Mr. Candler, in his interesting paper *On the Significance of some East Anglian Field Names* (*Norfolk Archæology*, vol. xi., part ii., p. 149), says, under the head of *Camping Close:*—"The famous old camping matches appear to have been encounters of an exceedingly ferocious character, and the game would stand very badly in the public opinion of a generation which can scarcely tolerate football played under Rugby Rules."

(6) "Sr John Elverich." It was the custom at this date (1539) to give the Clergy the title of Sir. The name of "John Elverich of North Elmham, Chaplain," occurs in a deed executed by Edmund Ferrour of Gressenhall, dated 19th July, 30th Henry VIII. (1538). Perhaps he was chaplain to Thomas, Lord Crumwell, or, from the fact that his name constantly occurs in the Churchwardens' Accounts, one of the clergy attached to the Church.

(7) "Rochetts." The difference between the rochet and the surplice is that the rochet has closer sleeves (the present Anglican

Bishops' rochet presents a striking departure from ecclesiastical tradition in this respect) and sometimes no sleeves (*Pugin*, p. 222). "Normādy canvas" was no doubt some linen substance prepared in Normandy for the purpose.

(8) "Yᶜ menor." The manner. Rich mould of any kind. In East Anglia to manner is to throw up brows of ditches or banks for mixing with dung or manure. Manner is a corruption of manure.—See Nall's *Glossary of East Anglia*, vol. ii., p. 598. "Cōveying away of yᵒ menor" means removing the soil.

(9) "Yᵉ feyer stede." The Fairsted was a piece of land abutting upon the churchyard at the east end, and, as it seems, close to or adjoining the Camping Close. Elmham Fair, abolished within the last few years, was an ancient institution. William Turbe, Bishop of Norwich, who was consecrated in 1146, confirmed to the priory all former grants of his predecessors, with the church at Elmham, and *the Fair*. It was formerly held each year on the 25th of March, the Feast of the Annunciation, but latterly on the 6th and 7th of April. It appears to have been removed at some time or other from the Fairsted to a piece of pasture at the southern end of the parish, to the west of the King's Head Inn, and called the Green Field. In 1593 there occurs the following entry of a burial in the Register Book :—"Thom̃s Crome of dearham who was kylled wᵗʰ a cart going from Elmham fayer ᵹ was buryed the 27 daye of Marche, 1593."

(10) "Chosen to be hys felow." The custom seems to have been that the churchwardens held office for two years. One retired each year, and the one who remained nominated his fellow.

Aᵒ Dm. 1540.

(11) "Iᵗ to my lord." Thomas, Lord Crumwell, Henry VIII.'s Vicegerent, who was in possession of the Elmham estate at this time.

(12) "Tᵍre natieᵍ" Terra nativa or copyhold land. For an explanation I again quote from Mr. Candler's paper (p. 147). Speaking of "Bond Meadow," he says that the word *bond* is in

common use "for a piece of *copyhold* land, which sometimes retains the old name after enfranchisement. The Latin equivalent of *land-bond* in manorial records is *terra nativa*, ter. nat., a very suggestive expression." It is here contrasted with *terra libera*, or freehold land.

(13) "To yᵉ howse of Carbrok." This was, no doubt, a payment made to the Commandery of Knights Hospitalers existing at Carbrooke, near Watton. It was in the archdeaconry of Norwich, the deanery of Breccles, the hundred of Wayland, and the honour of Clare. The house was founded previous to 1173, and was situated on the south side of the church of Great Carbrooke. Blomefield says that it consisted of a prior and fifteen knights. It had sixteen stalls in the church, and supported six boys at 40s. per annum. It possessed lands in fifteen parishes, of which no doubt Elmham was one.

(14) "To yᵉ pᵒor." The Prior of Norwich Cathedral Priory, which was founded by Herbert de Losinga, first Bishop of Norwich, 1091, and to which he appropriated the Rectory of Elmham Church.

(15) "Will Rūmer late deptyd." He was churchwarden in 1539, and died in the year of his office. The entry of his burial reads as follows in the Register:—"Will Rūmer, husbondman, was beryed yᵉ xxvj day of decembr (1539), wʰ was Christ friday and sent Stevyns day."

(16) "Mᵍ fferroʳ." The Ferrors or Ferrours were a family living in Gressenhall. Edmund Ferrour was lord of the manor of Harford in that parish in 30 Henry VIII. (1538). He had four sons, Thomas, John, Richard, and Robert. There was living in Elmham in 1523 Andrew Farror or Ferror, who by his will, dated 16th December, directed "that Margaret my wiff shall have all the Thyrm belynge tre and all the freute that come yʳ of." Mr. Carthew in the *Hundred of Launditch*, vol. iii., p. 220, is unable to give any

explanation as to the meaning of "Thyrm belynge tre." Possibly this Andrew is the "M⁹ fferoʳ" mentioned in the Accounts.

(17) "Payed to yᵉ bekyn." Beacon, from Saxon *Beacen* = signal. Camden derives it from *Beacman* = to give notice by a signal. It cannot be doubted but such fires were in use in the time of the Saxons, *i.e.*, somewhat earlier than the middle of the fifth century. As regards their form, Coke (*4th Institute*, c. xxv., p. 184) says, Before the reign of Edward III. they were but stacks of wood set up on high places, which were fired when the coming of enemies was descried; but in his reign pitch boxes, as now they be, were, instead of those stacks, set up. And this properly is a Beacon, though lighthouses, steeples, churches, castles, trees, come under the same denomination, and are called *signa marina, speculatoria*, or *signa maris*. According to Camden none but the King could erect any of those three, which was done by commission under the Great Seal, and later on by letters patent granted to the Lord High Admiral, who had power to erect all. By Act 8th Eliz. it is provided that the master and wardens and assistants of Depford Stroud may lawfully, at their costs, erect and set up beacons, marks, and signs for the sea on sea shores, and upon land near the sea coasts, whereby the danger may be avoided, and ships the better come to their ports. The money due or payable for the maintenance of beacons was called *beconagium*, which, as he says, was levied by the Sheriff of the county upon each hundred, as appears by an ordinance in manuscript for the county of Norfolk, issued to Robertus de Monte and Thomas de Bardolfe, who sat in Parliament as Barons, 14th Edward II. (*Archæologia*, vol. i., p. 1, by Professor Ward, Gresham Coll.) Beacons anciently were intended as signals for the better securing the kingdom from foreign invasion. On certain eminent places of the country were erected long poles, whereon were fastened pitch barrels, to be fired by night, and to smoke by day, to give notice in

a few hours to the whole kingdom of an approaching invasion. These served to communicate the alarming intelligence as rapidly as the modern invention of the telegraph. They were frequently used among the primitive Britons and Western Highlanders. Fingal instantly knew "the green flame, edged with smoke," to be a token of attack and distress. Hadley Church, near London, has an iron beacon-frame erected on a square tower at the west end; and I have myself seen one on the walls of Scarborough Castle.

(18) "Y* pctor of sent John." The Proctor of S. John, the agent or collector for the Hospital of S. John at Carbrooke. It was not unusual to describe a religious institution by the name of its patron saint.

(19) "To y* balyes." Simon Dethycke, whose name appears in the next entry of the Churchwardens' Accounts, was at this period baly, or bailiff, to Thomas Lord Crumwell's Manor of Nowers. He died in 1542, and was buried on the first day of March, having directed by his will that his body should be laid to rest in S. James' Chapel, on the south side of Elmham Church choir.

(20) "A shest (chest) to ley yn the Comon lyght." Wax was supplied out of the Church Fund for the light which was kept continually burning before the blessed sacrament on the high altar, and was provided, no doubt, for the use of side altars as well.

A° Dm. 1541.

(21) "Itm̃ for A Byble." In 1539 Grafton and Whitchurch printed, at London, the Bible in large folio, under the direction of Coverdale and patronage of Cranmer, containing some improvement of Matthew's translation: this is generally called the Great Bible. There were several editions of it, and particularly one in 1540, for which Cranmer wrote a preface, shewing that "Scripture should be had and read of the lay and vulgar people," hence this edition of 1540 is called Cranmer's Bible. In this year the curate and parishioners of every parish were required, by royal proclamation, to

I

provide themselves with the Bible of the largest size before the Feast of All Saints, under a penalty of 40s. a month; and all Ordinaries were charged to see that this proclamation was obeyed. It was "set up in the churches, where it might be read by the people, although it was not as yet used in the public service."—Procter, *Book of Com. Prayer.*

(22)  "Fre stone at Walsyngham Abbey." After the suppression of the Monasteries in 1536, it appears that the stones of Walsingham Abbey were sold. A load of them was bought by the Elmham Churchwardens for the repairs of the Church. Some of the richly-carved stones may be seen inserted in the wall over the north door.

(23)  "To see yͤ bells." The bells appear to have been taken down this year (1541) and sent to one Rugge of Norwich, whether to be re-cast, or for what purpose the Accounts do not record. They were re-hung the following year, 1542. There is no entry of their conveyance to Norwich, although the cost of removing them thither —some nineteen miles by road—must have been considerable. Mr. Rugge received 5s. as a part payment for whatever was done to them, but there is nothing to show that he was ever paid in full.

Aͦ Dm.
1542.

(24)  "Certen plate." The Reformation, to which Thomas, Lord Crumwell, was giving his whole mind, is begun in the Parish by the sale of some of the sacred vessels, the silver upon the Cross "yͭ the reliques wheryn," and the silver shoes "vpon yͤ brown rodes fete." It is difficult to decide what this may mean. The term "rood" is ordinarily applied to that figure or series of figures consisting of our Lord, His Blessed Mother, and S. John the Divine, placed in a loft or gallery at the entrance to the chancel of cathedrals or parish churches. If these three images formed the rood in Elmham Church, upon the feet of which of them were the silver shoes? I am not aware of any instance where the Saviour's feet are said to have been thus clad; I can only hazard a conjecture that they were used

on tho image which represented the Virgin Mary. Since writing the above, however, my attention has been called to the following :— Chauncy's *Hertfordshire* (quoted in Toulmin Smith's *Parish*, p. 494) gives an Inventory of the Church Goods of Welwyn in 1541, and in it occurs the following entry:—"Item a crosse w$^t$ Saint Mary and John w$^t$ the foote to the same belonging, of coper and gylt." It is, therefore, possible that these silver shoes formed a movable covering or casing put on to the feet (or base) of the brown rood or cross on special festivals.

Dr. Brewer, in *Phrase and Fable*, speaks of Rood Lane in London, so called from a rood or "Jesus on the Cross" placed there, and in Roman Catholic times held in great veneration. More generally the representation was of the Trinity; God the Father being represented as "the Ancient of days," fully clothed, with a nimbus round His head, holding the Cross, on which God the Son is represented as crucified, and God the Holy Ghost as descending in the form of a dove near the Saviour's head. The Virgin Mary and S. John are often placed near the principal figures.

> "Saviour, in Thine image seen,
> Bleeding on that precious *rood*."
> *Wordsworth.*

"By the rood" was an oath commonly in use in Roman Catholic times.

> "No, by the rood, not so."—*Shakespeare.*

See Webster's *Dictionary*.

(25) "y$^*$ lete fee." The "Leet" (Latin, lis, a lawsuit) or, as it was commonly called, the "Court Leet," was one of the courts held of right by the lord of a manor. In the Court Baron and Court Customary the *civil* business of the manor was transacted and new tenants were admitted. The Court Leet was the *criminal* or police court, where offences, such as encroachments, violations of the

manorial customs, and petty assaults, were presented and punished by fine. The presentments were usually made by the capital pledges of the tithings. By a law dating as far back as the time of King Henry I. every male of twelve years old and upwards was expected to enrol himself in a tithing or association of ten or twelve persons at least, each of whom was responsible for the good conduct of the rest. Each member of the tithing was a pledge for the rest, and one was called the capital or chief pledge. If one of the number offended and could not be produced, or if an offence was found to be concealed, the whole tithing was fined.

Long before this time the court leet had fallen into desuetude or, if held, into practical inefficiency in most places; its jurisdiction having been absorbed by the justices of the peace in the country, and by the aldermen or similar magistrates in the boroughs. Still the lords of the manors had the legal right to hold the court and to fine their tenants for non-attendance. It is probable that it was found mutually convenient for the tenants to pay to the lord a fixed annual sum to be free from the obligation of attendance, and from the fines which might be inflicted on them.

As the payment here of 24s., in the name of the "Leet Fee," implies the existence of the obligation to attend the court, and there is no hint of any fines being paid at any time, it seems most likely that the fee was the composition for non-attendance, if the lord still held the court, or, if the court were disused, an old customary payment originally made with that object.

A°. Dm. 1543.    (26) "A pursse ꝫ ij Combs yᵗ were Relyquys in yᵉ Chyrche." These were probably some of the relics mentioned before (note 24) as being concealed in the cross on the high altar. A marriage is entered in the Parish Register as solemnized in 1540, on 11th July, "wʰ was relique sōday;" in connection with which I am indebted to Dr. Jessopp for the following interesting information :—" Relic

Sunday is the first Sunday after S. Thomas' Day (8th July), *i.e.*, the Translation of S. Thomas the Martyr (Becket). In 1540 S. Thomas' Day fell on a Thursday; therefore Relic Sunday fell on the 11th, as stated in the Register."

(27) "Y* Town butts." If Englishmen have always been famous as sailors, the same (till the introduction of firearms) may be said of them as archers. In 1346 the battle of Cressy, and in 1356 Poitiers, was won by their prowess in this respect. Edward III. was very jealous of the honour of the bow. In 1363 he commanded the general practice of archery on Sundays and holidays, in lieu of ordinary rural sports, which were forbidden on pain of imprisonment. For the manufacture of bows yew was generally preferred; hence the reason, it has been said, why so many of our churchyards have yew trees planted in them. Several Acts were passed in the reign of Henry VII. for the encouragement and promotion of archery. One Act directed that butts should be erected and kept in repair in all townships, and that the inhabitants should practise shooting at them on holidays. Every able man, not being an ecclesiastic or a judge, was ordered to familiarise himself with the use of the long bow. Even the "godly Master Latimer" did not think it amiss to strongly advocate its use in his sermons before Edward VI. at S. Paul's Cross. The English victory at Flodden Field was due to the skill and courage of the archers; and entries in Edward VI.'s Journal in the British Museum show that he was fond of archery as an amusement. The Act for keeping up the butts was, generally speaking, respected in North Elmham, although the parish was once or twice fined for neglect.

(28) "Y⁰ obytee day of y* bñfactors." The obit was an anniversary office for the soul of the deceased on the day of his death. The anniversary of any person's death was called the obit; and to observe such a day with prayers and alms or other

I 2

commemoration was the keeping of the obit. In religious houses a register was kept, wherein were entered the obits or obitual days of founders or benefactors; this register was called the Obituary. The tenure of obit, or obituary, or chantry lands, is taken away by an Act of Edward VI.

**A°. Dm.**
**1544.**

(29) "Mr. Robert Nycholls." Amongst the Taverner Evidences given by Mr. Carthew in the *Hundred of Launditch*, the name of Sir Robert Nycholls, Clerk, occurs as witnessing the will of John Tav'ner, of Brysley, yeoman, dated 14th April, 1545. Also at a court in 23rd Henry VIII. it was presented that John Taverner, of Brisley, had alienated to Richard Sylvester, Clerk (Vicar of Elmham), a close called Seuston's in Elmham ; and Robert Nicholls, Clerk, executor of Sylvester's will, by which the close was devised to him, produced the will in court; but Taverner then refused to complete the surrender, and at the following court Nicholls released to him.

(30) "Y⁰ noysome wayes," the highways. The expression forcibly conveys an idea of their condition. They are "noysome" enough now, generally speaking, and in those days, no doubt, they were doubly "noysome."

(31) "Ry. Heywarde at yᵉ Crosse." He is thus described in the ancient Register Book, and in a note in my published copy of it, I have mentioned a piece of land in the parish, on the rising ground beyond the King's Head Inn and on the right hand side of the road running to Dereham, which still retains the name of "High Cross," and there I have supposed that the Parish Cross once stood. It is true that an entry farther on in the Churchwardens' Account Book in 1547 speaks "of yᵉ Hey Crosse to Ryborough ward," and this would seem to place it in exactly the opposite direction. But I think that it probably means that the lands referred to in the entry lay to the north or Ryburgh side of the cross. The piece of land

now called High Cross is memorable for the questionable act of Richard Warner, sometime owner of the Elmham Estate. Tradition says that he hired this land for the term of one crop, and sowed ACORNS. If men's good deeds survive them, so assuredly do their ill deeds.

(32) " Ye Kyngs Myll." This was, no doubt, a mill standing upon the site of that which is now known as Worthing Mill. The stream over which it is built separates Elmham from that parish. In a bundle of mutilated court-rolls, found by Mr. Carthew in the Muniment-room at Elmham Hall, the following appears :— " 3 Henry VIII. A presentment quod molendinarius de Kyngs- myll submerged pratum domini voc. Brodfen co quod obstupavit aquæ cum . . . . . et staks ad nocumentum tenentium domini, &c." In other words the miller is presented at the Manor Court for impeding the stream by placing stakes and other obstacles in it, and so causing the water to overflow and submerge a meadow called Brodfen. Brodfen is, no doubt, the same as Brodmarshe, which is repeatedly mentioned in the Churchwardens' Account Books. It lies in the direction of Beetley, and would become submerged by an overflow of water from the Worthing or King's Mill.

Since writing the above, my attention has been directed to a very able and interesting paper read by Mr. Clarke, of the Diocesan Registry, at Castleacre, on the 19th August, 1890, and what he there says seems to set the matter at rest. Speaking of Castleacre at the time of the dissolution of the monasteries, he makes the following remarks :—" I must mention a peculiar gift to the Convent. Henry de Rie, a companion of William the Conqueror, by will gave to the Priory (of Castleacre) his mill at Worthing, together with Thurston the miller, the miller's mother and brothers, and all their substance. This is a specimen of the feudal times. There is still a water-mill at Worthing." Mr. Clarke then goes on to say :—" On the 22nd

November, 1537, the Prior and some ten monks only (barely one-third of the supposed number in the convent) signed the deed surrendering their house and all its possessions "—the mill, of course, being amongst the number—"to King Henry VIII., and from that time the Convent ceased to exist." The mill, therefore, would thenceforth be appropriately spoken of as "the King's mill."

(33)  "When I rode to geyghton." When I rode to Gayton. This year and the next (1544-5) the churchwardens were summoned before Commissioners, at Gayton, Litcham, and East Dereham, on matters touching the Reformed Faith. The "vulgar tongue" was now ordered to be used in the Church Services, and Archbishop Cranmer received Henry VIII.'s command to make translations from the Latin. As a beginning, the English Litany, with which the people had been familiar for generations, was authorised for public worship.

A°. Dm.
1545.

(34)  "Yᵉ pson of Bylney." This was Nicholas Marshall, Rector of Bilney from 1525 to 1554.

(35)  "Yᵉ Soydyors (soldiers) yᵗ sholde have gone furth." This is the first mention of sending forth soldiers from the parish, and providing arms and clothing for them out of the Church Fund. The elements of disturbance were undoubtedly in the air. Mr. Rye, in his *History of Norfolk*, says:—"The temper was rising year by year. In 1540 one John Walker, of Griston, said, 'If three or four good fellows would ride in the night with every man a bell, and cry in every town they passed through, 'To Swaffham! To Swaffham!' by the morning there would be ten thousand assembled at least.' This intended rising was avowedly against the gentlemen. 'It would be a good thing,' said he, 'if there were only as many gentlemen in Norfolk as there were white bulls.' From after results it is clear that Walker was perilously near the truth as to the readiness to rise."

(36) "A Ratchett." The same word is used in the Accounts of the following year (1546), where a payment is made "to Margaret Croker for yᵉ mēdyng of A Ratchett." A ratchet is a piece of metal used to insert in the teeth of a wheel to stop its backward motion. This might be the implement intended in the first entry, but not in the second. To mend a ratchet would hardly be a woman's employment. In 1539 there is an entry of "six yards of Normandy Canvass for two rochetts," *i.e.*, ecclesiastical vestments (see note 7, p. 93). Perhaps it is to the mending of a rochet that the second entry refers.

(37) "For iij Gyrdles for yᵉ Albes." The albe is a loose and long ecclesiastical vestment, coming down to the feet, and having close-fitting sleeves reaching to the hands. Anciently it appears to have been made usually of linen, though in later times rich silks of different colours were frequently used; while, in the Russian Church, velvet is often employed. It was very commonly ornamented with square or oblong pieces of embroidery, called apparels; these were stitched on, or otherwise fastened to various parts of it, especially just above the feet and near the hands, where they had somewhat the appearance of cuffs. The Rubric of 1549 directs the use of "a white Albe plain," meaning, no doubt, a linen albe without apparels. The girdle is a cord or narrow band of silk or other material (usually white, with tassels attached). It is used for fastening the albe round the waist.—See Blunt's *Annotated Book of Common Prayer*.

(38) "Yᵉ laten Censors." Laten or latten is a fine kind of brass or bronze used in the middle ages for crosses, candlesticks, and censers. The censer is a vessel in which incense is burned.

"Her thoughts are like the fume of frankincense,
Which from a golden censer forth doth rise."
*Spenser.*

Aᵒ. Dm.
1546.

(39) "Añe Taûner of Bresesele." This must have been Anne

Taverner, wife of John of North Elmham and Brisley. She was the daughter of . . . . Crow of East Bilney, and died in or before 1557.

(40) "Yᵉ Chyrche gate plow." I imagine that this must have been a plough kept in common use, near the church, for the plough-men on Plough Monday, and that the 17s. 4d. here mentioned as being in the custody of Sir John Elveriche, clerk, was the sum, or some portion of it, collected in the parish on the previous anniversary. Plough Monday was the Monday next after Twelfth Day, when in the north of England ploughmen drew a plough from door to door, and begged plough money to drink; they then ploughed two furrows across in a base court or other place near houses. In other parts of England if any ploughmen, after their day's work, came to the kitchen-hatch with a goad or whip and cried, "Cock in the pot" before the maids said, "Cock on the dunghill," then they gained a cock for Shrove Tuesday. Tusser thus alludes to this quaint custom :—

> "Plough Monday, next after that Twelfth-tide is past,
> Bids out with the plough, the worst husband is last;
> If ploughmen get hatchet, or whip to the shreene,
> Maids loseth their cocke, if no water be seen."

(41) "Holy Rode daye." The 14th September.

(42) "A gret lantorn to bear lyght before yᵉ Sacramēt." This was, no doubt, intended for procession through the streets when the reserved Sacrament was carried to the sick.

(43) "Yᵉ red Cope." A kind of full long cloak, of a semi-circular shape, reaching to the heels, and open in front, thus leaving the arms free below the elbows. It is worn over either the albe or the surplice.—See Blunt's *Annotated Book of Common Prayer.*

(44) "In yᵉ quere by the Sepulchre." This was on the north side of the chancel, and was a place where the Blessed Sacrament was

solemnly reserved from Good Friday to Easter Day. There were two kinds used for this purpose in the old churches: 1, Permanent, built in the north walls of the choir or chancel, and adorned with rich ornamental covering and appropriate imagery; 2, Composed of frame work and rich hangings, set up for the occasion. There are few parochial churches which are not provided with a tomb on the north side of the chancel, which served for the sepulchre, and was adorned on these occasions with hangings and other decorations. Devout persons erected these tombs with the especial intention of their serving for the sepulchre, that those who came to visit it in Holy Week might be moved to pray for their souls. When a *Rationale of the Rights and Ceremonies of the English Church* was set forth in the reign of Henry VIII., the following exposition of the sepulchre was given:—" And on that day (Good Friday) is prepared and well adorned the Sepulchre, in remembrance of His sepulture, which was prophesied by the prophet Esaias to be glorious; wherein is laid the image of the Cross and the most blessed Sacrament: to signify that there was buried no corpse or body that could be putrified or corrupted, but the pure and undefiled Body of Christ, without spot of sin, which was never separated from the Godhead, that, as David expressed it in the 15th Psalm, it could not see corruption; nor death could not detain or hold Him, but He should rise again, to our great hope and comfort. And therefore the Church adorns it with lights, to express the great joy they have of that glorious triumph over death and the devil."—*Collier*, vol. ii., pp. 197-8.

A sepulchre still (1868) remains in Long Melford Church, Suffolk. An old MS. in Neal's *Views of Churches* gives the following description of the ceremony of the sepulchre, as it was practised in that church:—" In the quire there was a fair painted frame of timber, to be set up about Maunday Thursday, with holes for a number of fair tapers to stand in before the Sepulchre, and to be lighted in service time. Sometimes it was set overthwart the quire, before the High Altar; the Sepulchre being alwaies placed, and finely garnished, at the north end of the High Altar; between that and Mr. Clopton's little chappel there in a vacant place of the wall; I think *upon the tomb of one of his ancestors*," &c.

### Antiquities of Durham Abbey.

Good Friday.—"The adoration of the Cross being ended, two monks carried the Cross to the Sepulchre with great reverence; (which was set up *that morning* on the north side of the quire nigh unto the High Altar, before y^e service time) and there laid it in the said Sepulchre with great devotion, with another picture of our Saviour Christ, in whose breast they enclosed with great reverence the most Holy and Blessed Sacrament of y^e Altar, censing and praying to it upon their knees a great space; setting two tapers lighted before it, which burned till Easter Day in the morning."

Easter Day.—"There was in the Church of Durham a very solemn service upon Easter Day between three and four o'clock in the morning, in honour of the Resurrection, when two of the eldest monks of the quire came to the Sepulchre set up on Good Friday after the Passion, all covered with red velvet and embroidered with gold, out of which with great reverence they took an extreme beautiful Image of our Saviour, representing the Resurrection, with a Cross in His hand, in the breast whereof was inclosed in the brightest crystal, the Holy Sacrament of the altar, through which crystal the Blessed Host was conspicuous to the beholders. Then after the elevation of y^e said picture, carried by y^e s^d two monks upon a velvet cushion all embroidered, singing the anthem of *Christus Resurgens*, they brought it to the High Altar," &c.

The Service connected with the Sepulchre appears to have been conducted in England with great and edifying solemnity.—*Pugin*, 3rd ed., pp. 206-7-8.

(45) "Chantryes and ppetuytyes." Chantries and hospitals dissolved and granted to the Crown by 37th Henry VIII., c. 4. The chantry was an endowed chapel where masses were sung or said daily for the souls of the donors. Perpetuities would, no doubt, represent endowments of all kinds for religious purposes.

(46) "Yᵉ best Canapye." A rich cloth or covering suspended as a hood over the Blessed Sacrament on the Altar, or borne over it when carried in processions. It was made of velvet, silk, or cloth of gold, and richly embroidered with appropriate devices, and borne by four, six, eight, or twelve staves of wood or silver, to which small bells were usually attached. A canopy of state was also borne over the hearse in funerals of noble persons. Colours—Roman use white, but in French and Flemish churches, generally red. In England both colours were used indifferently. In the Church of Holy Trinity, Melford, Suffolk, there was "A cloth of *blue* silk to bear over the Sacrament, with chalices of gold embroidered thereon; the gift of Robert Miller." In the parish church of Faversham, Kent, we find "Item, a canapy clothe, pounsyd, garneyshd about with purpill velvett, with tascellys of red sylke. Item, a canapy for the Sacrament, of crimson sarsanet, with knoppis of golde and tascellys of red sylke. Item, 2 canapyes of lawne for the Sacrament, one with knoppis of coppir, and gret knoppis of golde, wroughte with the nedyll, and tascellys of red sylke; and the other hath none."— Jacob's *History of Faversham*; Pugin's *Glossary of Ecclesiastical Ornaments*, 3rd ed., pp. 56, 57.

(47) "Yᵉ Crosse clothe of sylk." This was a veil for the cross which stood upon the High Altar. The custom of hanging these veils in the English churches was explained in the following manner in a *Rationale* set forth in 1541 :—"The covering of the Cross and

images in Lent, with the uncovering of the same at the Resurrection, signifies not only the darkness of infidelity, which covered the face of the Jews in the O. T., but also the dark knowledge they had of Christ, Who was the perfection and end of the Law ; and not yet opened until the time of His death and resurrection.  And the same partly is signified by the Veil which hid the secret place of the *Sanctum Sanctorum* from the people, and in the time of Christ's Passion was opened, that all men might see it and have a ready entrance thereinto."—Collier's *History*, vol. ii., p. 197.

**(48)**  " Y* Cope."  See note 43, p. 106.

**A° Dm.**
**1547.**

**(49)**  " Crocks and Trenchers."  Earthenware cups and wooden plates.  These may have been for use on Hallowmas night, the festivities of which appear to have been now abolished, and so, there being no further need of cups and plates, they were sold.  Mr. Carthew thinks that "crocks " may mean crooks for sheep, but I cannot see any reason for this supposition.

**(50)**  " My lady Hastyngs."  It seems probable that she was Elizabeth, daughter of Sir Hugh Hastings, who died 32nd Henry VIII., 1540.  She died 1580, having married Hamon Le Strange, of Hunstanton, co. Norfolk, Esq., lord of Gressenhall and East Lexham, co. Norfolk, *jure uxoris*.  He died October, 22nd Elizabeth, 1580.  Her sister, Anne Hastings, married William Brown, Esq., second son of Sir Anthony Brown, K.G., lord of Elsing, co. Norfolk, *jure uxoris*.  Sir George Hastings, Sir Hugh's father, possessed a water-mill in Elmham, called *Gryndmille*, and lands belonging.

**(51)**  " ij Tables for Aulters."  These may possibly have been intended for the chapels of SS. John and James, on the north and south sides of the chancel.  The removal of stone altars had been partially begun, although no peremptory order was issued respecting them till November, 1550.

(52) "Oʳ late souⁱayn Lord kyng Henry the viijᵗʰ." He died January 28th, 1547.

(53) "A Monstrant of Sylu." Latin *montro*, to show or exhibit. The monstrance is a transparent pyx, or box, in which, in the Romish Church, the consecrated wafer, or Host, is held up to view before the congregation. Host = *hostia* (victim), and is the name given to altar bread before consecration. It also signifies the blessed sacrament itself.—*Pugin*, p. 158.

(54) "A payer of Sensors wᵗ yᵉ shype of Sylu." These are all vessels for holding incense.

(55) "A payer of Paxes of Sylu." Parker, in his *Concise Glossary of Architecture*, says:—" Pax (Latin), Paxbrede, a small tablet having on it a representation of the Crucifixion, or some other Christian symbol, offered to the congregation in the Romish Church to be kissed in the celebration of the Mass :· it was usually of silver or other metal, with a handle at the back, but was occasionally of other materials; sometimes it was enamelled and set with precious stones. The pax was introduced when the *osculum pacis*, or kiss of peace, was abrogated on account of the confusion which it entailed."

(56) "A payer of Chalyce." The holy sacrament had hitherto been delivered to the laity in one kind only; the cup had been denied them. In December of this year (1547, 1st Edward VI.) an Act of Parliament was passed, with the unanimous approval of the convocation of the clergy, converting the mass into a communion, and requiring that the holy sacrament should be delivered to the people, and under both kinds.—Berens, *History of the Prayer Book.* Chalices had therefore to be supplied.

(57) "Hey Crosse to Ryborough warde."—See note 31, p. 102.

Aº Dm. 1548.

(58) "Itm̄ rec̄ for yᵉ Clothes yᵗ hange before yᵉ roode lofte wᵗ other small steyned clothes & yᵉ ymages." The Canon required all pictures, reliefs, or statues of saints to be covered up during Lent.

This was done by coverings of linen or silk, on which symbols of the Passion were sometimes painted. "Steyned clothes for Lent," as these were called, are very common items in old church inventories. In wealthy churches each important image had its own set of "steyned clothes;" the most important of all being that which was used to cover the great rood on the choir screen. The whole east end of the sanctuary was concealed by a curtain called the Lenten Veil, which hung from wall to wall of the sanctuary, a few feet to the west of the high altar. In many cases the iron hooks which supported this curtain may still be seen in the north and south walls. (Professor Middleton, before the Cambridge Antiquarian Society. See *John Bull*, December 14th, 1889, p. 819.) "Yᵉ ymages." In the first year of Edward VI., 1547-8, an ecclesiastical visitation was carried out for the purpose of removing images and compelling the use of the English tongue in the Church Services.

(59) "Yᵉ Chapell of Becke." I am indebted to Mr. Clarke, of the Diocesan Registry, for the following account of the Hospital to to which this Chapel was attached:—"Bec (or Beck) Hospital was in Billingford, and was founded in the reign of Henry III. (circa 1222) by one William de Bec, who appointed Richard, his chaplain, Master thereof. It had thirteen beds for receiving poor travellers every night, and also a chapel dedicated to S. Thomas the Martyr. The chapel appears to have been subsequently re-dedicated to S. Paul, probably in the year 1538, when Henry VIII. by proclamation caused the name of S. Thomas of Canterbury to be expunged from the Calendar.

In 37th Henry VIII. (1546) the Hospital, with its messuages, lands, &c., in Billingford, Hoe, East Dereham, Swanton Morley, Brisley, Gateley, North Elmham, and several other parishes, was granted to one John Curson and his heirs.

There is at the present time a farm-house at Billingford called Beck Hall, in the occupation of Mr. Robert Hudson.

The late Mr. J. G. Nichols, in his *Pilgrimage to Walsingham and Canterbury*, speaking of Walsingham says: that "the principal road by which the pilgrims travelled thither from the south passed by Newmarket, Brandon, and Fakenham, and is still known as the Palmer's Way and the Walsingham Green Way, and that another great road led from the east through Norwich and Attleborough by *Bec Hospital*, where gratuitous accommodation for thirteen pilgrims was provided every night."

"I have not at present," Mr. Clarke goes on to say, "traced Walsingham Way from Elmham. It may have passed through Great and Little Ryburgh, or through Guist to Pensthorpe, and from thence to Fakenham, on the north side of which it passed by the late turnpike road through East Barsham and Houghton to Walsingham. There was a road in Elmham called Walsingham Way."

(60) "A Byble & yᵉ paraphrasys of Erasmᵒ." On the accession of Edward VI. (January 28th, 1547) measures were taken to set up the "Great Bible" in the churches, together with a translation of the Paraphrase of Erasmus on the Gospels and Acts of the Apostles, to be studied by the clergy. For the "Great Bible," see note 21 ante, p. 97.

(61) "Putte ynto yᵉ poore folcks Cheste at yᵉ quere doore." Cunningham, in his *Growth of English Industry and Commerce*, says, p. 479 :—"A considerable step in advance was made in the year (1536) of the suppression of the monasteries. It was found that the existing Acts (that able-bodied vagrants should be publicly whipped and sent to the place of their birth) could not be enforced, because there was no fund for the relief of the impotent poor, nor for the employment of the able-bodied when they returned to the places

K

where they ought to be maintained ; there were besides no sufficient instructions as to the way in which tramps should repair to their proper districts. A beggar who was tramping homewards at the rate of ten miles a day was to be relieved ' upon the sight of his letters given him at the time of his whipping,' and the officers of all towns and villages were to keep the poor by way of voluntary and charitable alms ; while they were to set the able-bodied to work, so that they might maintain themselves. The churchwardens were to gather the alms with boxes on Sundays, Festivals, and Holy Days, so that the poor, impotent, lame, sick, feeble, and diseased might be sufficiently provided for, and not have to go about and beg."

(62) "Itm̄ in Chargs at Walsynghm̄, &c." This was the Commission for removing images, asserting the royal supremacy, and compelling the use of the English tongue.

(63) "Ye Table at yᵉ Hygh Aulter." By this it would seem that in the first instance and before its removal to the midst of the choir, a table was placed in front of the High Altar (which had now ceased to be used) for Holy Communion, unless, indeed, a credence table is here intended.

A° Dm.
1549.

(64) "Y° pte of Chryste Chyrche." Norwich Cathedral Priory, founded by Herbert de Losinga, Bishop of Norwich, and endowed by him with the rectory and the advowson of Elmham Vicarage. It would appear that the expense of certain requirements for the church was shared between the church fund and the priory.

(65) "For yᵉ order of the new (Service)." The order of council of 1548. This was the first Prayer-book of Edward VI. Certain bishops and divines, with Archbishop Cranmer, received authority to compile it. The "Order of Communion," preparatory to a more complete book, had been already issued in March, 1547. The Commissioners met again at Windsor, the 1st September, 1548, and before the end of the year presented the new Prayer-book to the

king to be laid before Parliament. It was ordered to be taken into use on and after the Feast of Pentecost (June 9th) in the following year.

(66) "All Chantryes and such other." All colleges, chantries, and free chapels were given to the king by Act of Parliament, 1 Edward VI., c. 14.

A° Dm.
1550.

(67) "Antyphoners, Grayles, legends, Masbokes." The Antiphon was an Anthem or Psalm sung alternately by a choir or congregation, divided into two parts, and is the most ancient form of church music. The Antiphonarium contained the Antiphons sung in the services of the Hours, arranged for the respective days and hours : it gradually collected other portions, the invitatories, hymns, responses, verses, collects, and little chapters, *i.e.*, the portions sung in the Service of the Canonical Hours.

The Grayle, or Gradale, or Graduale, was the "Antiphonarium" for the Service of High Mass, containing the portions to be sung by the choir, and was so called from certain phrases after the Epistles, sung " in gradibus."

The Legends or Legenda contained the Lections read at the Matin Offices, whether taken from Scripture, Homilies of the Fathers, or Lives of the Saints.—*Procter.*

The Mass Book contained the Service of the Holy Eucharist. In 1542 a Committee of Convocation was appointed to examine and reform all Mass Books, Antiphoners, and Portuisses or Breviaries. (The Breviary contained the several Services for the Canonical Hours:—1, Nocturns, used before daylight; 2, Lauds, early morning; 3, Prime, a later Morning Service ; 4, Tierce, at nine o'clock a.m. ; 5, Sext, at noon ; 6, Nones, at three o'clock p.m. ; 7, Vespers, or Evening Service). All mention of the Bishop of Rome's name, all apocryphas, feigned legends, superstitious orations, collects, versicles, and responses, names and memories of all Saints not mentioned in

Scripture, or authentical doctors (what judge was to decide who were "authentical doctors" and who were not, it seems difficult to understand), were to be abolished and put out of the same books and calendars. In 1549 appeared another Royal Proclamation, which aimed at destruction itself. After reciting that a Book of Common Prayer had been agreed upon and commanded to be used throughout the realm, it goes on to say that "dyvers unquyette and evile disposed persons had noysed and bruited abrode, that they sholde have agayne their olde Lattene Service;" we therefore "have thought goode, and neverthelesse straightly to commaunde and charge you (the Bishops) that immediately upon the receipt hereof, you do commaunde the deane and prebendaries of the cathedrall Churche, the parson, vicar, or curatte, and churchewarden of everie parishe within youre diocesse, to bring and deliver unto you or your deputie, at soche convenient place as you shall appoynt, all antiphoners, missales, grayles, processionalles, manuells, legendes, pies (a pie, pye, or pica is the Romish directory for devotional services), portasies, jornalles and ordinalles, and all other bokes of service, and that you take the same bokes into your handes, and then so deface and abolyshe that they never after may serve to anie soche use as they were provided for." The havoc was terrible. Monasteries were . suppressed and their libraries destroyed; churches and private houses were ransacked. Ships laden with these books carried them over sea. Candlesticks were scoured and boots rubbed with them; grocers and soapboilers made use of them, a single merchant buying two noble libraries for forty shillings a piece. The wild passions of Edward's days knew not their value, nor thought of the regret with which after ages would feel their loss.—*Maskell*.

(68)   "Y⁰ Chapell of y⁰ Beck." See note 59, ante, p. 112.

(69)   "Y⁰ Towne Carre lyeng w'in y⁰ p⁰cyncts of Betele." Carr is a wood or grove on a swampy soil, generally of alders; probably

from Gael. "garan," a thicket, also underwood. Wel. "carȝ," a thicket, brake (Nall's *Glossary*). Blomefield, in *Hist. of Norf.*, speaks of an "alder carr."

(70) "Yᵉ stocks." This is the first mention of stocks in the parish. In 1551, it will be seen that a new "payer" had to be supplied "to punysshe wᵗ trāsgressours Ageynste yᵉ Kyngs Maiesties lawes."

(71) "Ye settyng forthe of yᵉ Soudyours of Northelmhm̄ ⁊ others." This was the year (1549) of Ket's Rebellion. Twelve men of Elmham were equipped out of the Church Fund with bows, arrows, swords, and daggers, and sent forth to the camp at Mousehold Heath, on the north side of Norwich, where they formed a part of the Hundred of Launditch contingent. One of them returned home "hurt at yᵉ ffyrste skyrmysshe." Eight are mentioned as tarrying at the camp, and, no doubt, were present on the 27th August, when the rebels were routed. The cause of the rising was as follows:—The depreciation of the currency had been followed by its necessary consequence, a proportionate advance in the price of saleable commodities. The value of land rose with the value of produce. Rents of farms had been doubled and tripled in the course of a few years; but the wages of the working classes were not raised in proportion. The demand for labour was lessened, and, therefore, the price of labour sank. Experience had proved that the growth of wool was more profitable than the growth of corn, and the result was that the tillage of the soil was discouraged, and more pasture was created. In most counties thousands of labourers were out of work, and the distress which followed was increased by the doings of the landlords. In former times, especially on ecclesiastical estates, considerable portions of land were allotted for the common use of the labourers and the poor. The present owners, however, by repeated enclosures, added wastes and commons to farms, thus cutting off a

K 2

valuable source of support from the poor.    Lands were frequently
let to "leasemongers," or middlemen, at advanced rents, who
oppressed both farmer and cottager to benefit themselves.    The new
form of religion, too, added to the discontent.    The new proprietors
of Church lands paid less attention to the wants of the poor, who
complained that not only were they worse off temporarily, but were
compelled to practise a religion alien to their feelings and habits.
The new Service seemed but dead and dull after the music and
ceremony of the High Mass.    So sorely aggrieved were the people, that,
upon the new Liturgy being read in the Church of Samford Courtenay,
Devon, on Whitsunday (10th June, 1549), the next day the parishioners compelled the clergyman to resume the old Service.    Thus
matters combined for a serious rising.    Wiltshire, Sussex, Surrey,
Hampshire, Buckinghamshire, Kent, Gloucestershire, Somersetshire,
Suffolk, Essex, Warwickshire, Hertfordshire, Leicestershire, Wor-
cestershire, and Rutlandshire rose in revolt, which, after giving no
inconsiderable trouble to the authorities, was quelled.    In Oxfordshire,
however, Norfolk, Cornwall, and Devonshire, the rising assumed
a more dangerous shape.    It was only suppresed by aid of foreign
troops, bands of adventurers raised in Italy, Spain, and Germany to
serve in the war against Scotland.    In Norfolk the first rising was at
Attleborough, and, though contemptible in its origin it became the
nucleus round which the discontented of the neighbouring parishes
ranged themselves.    Ket,* a tanner, and the lord of three manors in
the county, became the leader.    He planted his standard on the
summit of Mousehold Hill, near Norwich, and erected for himself a
throne, under a spreading oak, which he called the Oak of Reforma-

---

* Mr. Rye, in his interesting *History of Norfolk*, says that the Kets were an old
and fairly wealthy family at Wymondham.    Thomas Ket, in 1570, betrayed the
conspiracy against the Norwich Strangers, and Francis Ket, in 1588, was burnt for
blaspheming Christ.

tion, and established Courts of Chancery, King's Bench, and Common Pleas, in imitation of the Courts at Westminster. In his proclamations he complained that the commons were being ground down, by the rich; that a new Service had been forced on people, opposed to their consciences; and declared, that if he and his people had taken up arms, it was only to place trusty counsellors round the king during his minority, and to remove those "who confounded things sacred and profane, and regarded nothing but the enriching of themselves with the public treasure, that they might riot in it during the public calamity." Obeyed by 20,000 followers, he treated all offers of pardon with scorn ; and when the Marquis of Northampton had entered Norwich with 1000 English horse and a body of Italians under Malatesta, he attacked the city, set one part on fire, killed the Lord Sheffield and an hundred men, and compelled the Marquis and his followers to retire out of the county. The Council, alarmed, re-called the troops from Scotland ; and the gentlemen of the neighbouring counties were ordered by royal proclamation to join the king's forces. The command was given first to the Protector Somerset, and afterwards to the Earl of Warwick. He, with 8,000 men, of whom 2,000 were Germans, forced his way into Norwich, but so incessant were the attacks of Ket's men, and so lavish were they of their lives, that they often drove the gunners from their batteries, burst open the gates, and fought with the soldiers in the streets. The Earl commanded his men to swear on their swords that they would never abandon the place, and at length was able to dislodge the enemy from their positions of vantage. Compelled by want of provisions, Ket descended the hill. In Dussingdale he was overtaken by the Royal army, his followers were broken by a cavalry charge, and about 2,000 perished in the action and pursuit. The remainder, however, surrounded themselves with a rampant of waggons and a trench fortified with stakes, and to an offer of pardon replied that they knew the fate which awaited them, and that it was better to perish by sword than by halter. The Earl of Warwick, however, still apprehensive of the result, persuaded them to accept the conditions, and the insurrection ended in the hanging of Ket on Norwich Castle, his brother on the steeple of Wymondham Church, and of nine others on the nine branches of the Oak of Reformation. To these events we owe the appointment of Lords Lieutenants of Counties, to whom were entrusted the duties of inquiring into treason, insurrections, and riots, with authority to levy men and lead them against the enemies of the king. (See Lingard's *Hist. Eng.*, 5th ed., vol. v., pp. 284 to 291.)

The account of the setting forth of the Elmham men in the Churchwardens' Book is very interesting. One Richard Watson appears to have been in command of the company, and the parish constable went with them to the camp. The Church Fund, besides equipping them with arms, supplied carts, and horses, and harness; and a plentiful stock of provisions was ordered, such as firkins of "beare," "garleck," "oynnyngs" (onions), "salt," "bredd," "ffysshe" (fish), "musterd," &c., &c. While the bread-winners were away, their wives were not forgotten at home.

(72) "M⁹ vycar And other Co⁹mãded to be before yᵉ kyngs Co⁹myssyoners." This and the following entry no doubt refer to the ordering of the new service. "My lord of Canterburye" is Archbishop Cranmer.

(73) "yᵉ hye Aulter." The High Altar appears now to have been removed, and set up table-wise in the midst of the choir. The "Aulter stone" was taken away, and a "mynystryng" table, which would seem to have been in addition to the Altar, was provided.

(74) "Ye Saulter boks, &c." The Act of Uniformity, 2 and 3 Edw. VI., c. 1.

A° Dm.
1551.

**75)** "Y° bokes of y° old s⁹ruyce." "M⁹ Vicar" is again ordered to appear before the Commissioners, who sat this time at Litcham, and to bring with him all the old books, *i.e.*, the Missals and Service Books to be given up by order of Council, December, 1549.

**(76)** "Itm̃ for A payer of Stocks." See note 70, p. 117.

**(77)** "S⁹rten holes in y° walls of the Chansell." Where, perhaps, the High Altar and the Sepulchre had been.

**(78)** "Itm̃ for y° setyng of A longe forme, &c." After the Altar was brought down into the choir the communicants sat round it on a form during the celebration of the Holy Communion.

**(79)** "A Stulppe." Stulp ; a short, stout post, used to mark a boundary, or driven into the ground for any purpose.—Webster's *Dictionary*.

**(80)** "Verdells." East Anglian for the hooks which rest upon the hinges of a gate. They are of two kinds, short and long verdells.

A° Dm.
1552.

**(81)** "The falls of y° monye." The depreciation of money this year (1552) causes a loss in the Church Accounts of £2. 10s. 11d. Mr. Carthew thinks that this was owing to the Act of Parliament forbidding usury. Another reason may have been the debasing of the currency, begun by Henry VIII., and repeated by the Protector Somerset on even a more damaging scale.

A° Dm.
1553.

**(82)** "Y° olde wall." Mr. Carthew is of opinion that this wall had possibly some connection with Bishop Spencer's Castle, the ruins of which are close by, on the north side of the Church.

**(83)** "An Inuentarye of y° Chyrche goods." The second Prayer-book of Edward VI.

**(84)** "Y° booke of y° new s⁹ruys." The second Prayer-book of Edward VI. A revision of the first Prayer-book having been now (1552) ordered, a second Act of Uniformity, with the revised book (commonly called the second book of Edward) attached,

was passed by Parliament on April 6th, and was directed to come
into use on the Feast of All Saints following. There is no proof
that it ever received the sanction of Convocation, though it is
unlikely that Cranmer would have permitted it to appear in
Parliament without it.

(85)   "Y⁰ Chyrche Goods wᵗ yᵉʳ Inuetarye of y⁰ same." Mr.
Carthew says that the commissions issued, in 1551, to seize the
jewels and rich vestments of the churches into the king's hands
were so dishonestly executed that other commissions were appointed
in 1553.

A⁰ Dm.
1556.

(86)   "A⁰ Dm̃ 1556." During the reign of Queen Mary, the
accounts are entered in the Churchwardens' Book for this year only;
the preceding years, 1554 and 1555, are omitted. Mary succeeded
to the Crown in July, 1553, and in the October following an Act
was passed suppressing King Edward's Liturgy, and restoring that
in use in the time of Henry VIII. The Act provided that the
clergy should be at liberty till the 20th December to use either the
old or the new service. After that date the old service was
imperatively enjoined. 1556 was the first year of the Marian
Persecution.

(87)   "The taske booke," i.e., tax book; and so post "for ellmhm̃
taske," Elmham tax.

(88)   "Questmen—the generall." There is an interesting passage
illustrating these two words in Toulmin Smith's The Parish, p. 70,
2nd edition. He says, "As Sidesmen are often mentioned together
with Churchwardens, this is the proper place to remark that a part
of what has more lately been reckoned as one duty of the churchwardens—the making of presentments—was formerly that of the
Sidesmen only." The authority of Bishop Gibson cannot be
considered as other than conclusive on such a point. He tells us
that—so far as they had to do with the church—" Churchwardens

were, by their original office, only to take care of the goods, repairs, and ornaments of the church, for which purpose they have been reputed a Body Corporate for many hundred years, as appears by the Ancient Register of Writs. But the business of presenting was devolved upon them by Canons and Constitutions of a more modern date. The ancient method was not only for the clergy, but the body of the people within such a district to appear at Synods, or, as we now call them, General Visitations (for what we now call Visitations were really the annual Synods). And the way was, to select a certain number to give information upon oath concerning the manners of the people. But afterwards when the body of the people began to be excused from attending, it was directed that four, six, or eight should appear, together with the clergy, to represent the rest, and to be the *testes synodales*," that is Synodsmen. "And this," says he, "is evidently the original of that office which our Canons call the Office of Sidesmen, or assistants—sometimes Questmen."

According to this, the "queste men" would be those elected to answer the Archdeacon's "quest" or enquiry at the Synod as to the spiritual condition of the parish in the matter of immorality and other offences which came under the cognizance of his court.

(89) "Yᵉ englyshe books." These were removed because the Service in Latin was now again in use.

A° Dm. 1561. (90) "James Taverner." He was the fifth son of John Taverner of North Elmham, and was of Hadlands in the same parish, and died in 1604, having married Grace, daughter and heir of John Russell of Wyghton, Norfolk, and relict of Edmund Bedingfield. For some account of this ancient family, I will refer the reader to the Elmham (1538) Register, lately published. James Taverner bore a notorious and conspicuous part in Elmham affairs.

(91) "Stone Caryeng from the tower." Bishop Spencer's Castle, the ruins of which were no doubt further dismantled for the purpose

of supplying stone for church repairs. Such history, scant though it be, as can be gleaned of this is very interesting. It was known in early times as *The Place*, or site of the Manor of Nowers, in Elmham. Two original charters in the muniment-room of Elmham Hall, temp. Edw. I. and II., are endorsed respectively : (1) "This Deyde conteyneth *The Place* in . . . in occupat Thome Franklyn (modo vocat le grange dni Henrici Crumwell ; " and (2) "This is the dede of the very mansion house of Roger Martyn called *The Place* in Elmham (which Franklyn occupieth)." To which is added, "de feodo Noeres." In 1867, when the present writer was appointed to the parish, all that was left of the ruins of this mansion, the site of which now forms a part of the vicarial glebe, was a portion of a tower and a few pieces of old wall just standing above ground. He has at length succeeded in excavating, partly with his own hands, what appears to be the whole building. A castle has risen from the soil. Blomefield, in his *Hist. Norf.*, says, "In the 11th year of Rich. II., Henry Spencer, Bishop (of Norwich), had a license to embattle and make a castle of his manor-house." The name has now undergone a change : it is no longer known as *The Place*, but as the Tower Hills. The outside walls are evidently of very great age, and one would venture to think long anterior to Bishop Spencer's time, the end of the fourteenth century, indeed it is difficult to say how far back they may not be traced. Mr. Carthew was of opinion that there was an Episcopal residence here at a much earlier date than the time of Henry Spencer, who simply enlarged and strengthened the building. It is not unlikely that some of the Elmham bishops inhabited it. Portions of the walls and of the stone-work still standing in the interior evidently point to the fourteenth century, but the greater part of the exterior gives one the impression of much greater age. During the excavations, many curious objects came to light. Human skulls and bones were found almost to any amount; one skull was mortared into the wall; three skeletons were in layers above each other, one of them having the arm bones extended upwards. Was it that the poor wretch had undergone the agonies of the rack? Several yellow, black, and plain tiles, with the glazing very perfect; pieces of stained glass, some having a bishop's mitre very rudely designed upon them; deer's tynes, two large thimbles, one copper and the other brass; part of a terra cotta Roman lamp (the site of the castle is on a Roman encampment, and Roman bricks and tiles appear in the walls); an old spur, the copper leg of what appears to have been a crucible, a dagger which came to pieces as soon as exposed to the air, and tradesmen's tokens temp. Elizabeth—all these have been discovered at one time or another with various fragments of mediæval pottery.

Henry le Spencer, commonly known as the warrior Bishop of Norwich, was consecrated in 1370, and was a man of some note, though by no means in all respects note-worthy. He was a soldier before he became a Bishop, and, after donning the mitre, the spirit of a soldier still possessed him, and could not be extinguished. Mr. Walter Rye speaks of him as "the grandson of the vile favourite of Edward II." Like the charger which he bestrode, he was ever snuffing the battle from afar, and to gather together his retainers and speed forth on some military expedition, or quell some popular disturbance, came to him as the ordinary routine of his life. The imposition of the poll tax in 1381 was the cause of no little opposition, and its resistance resulted eventually in the determination that "no tenant should do service or custom to the lords." The rebellion was led in the eastern counties by one John Litester, generally supposed to have been a Norwich dyer, and the chief aiders and abettors were Seth, Trunch, and Cubit. Success was first of all upon the side of the rioters, who compelled the Earl of Suffolk to fly in disguise, and put certain of the gentry whom they captured to menial offices. No sooner, however, did the news of the rising reach the ears of the warrior bishop than, smarting under the remembrance of the corporeal thrashing which he had received at the hands of the Commons of Lynn in 1377, he attacked the rebels with a mere handful of troops at Cambridge, seized and beheaded some of the leaders at Icklingham, and thence, advancing upon Norwich, was joined by a strong body of nobility and gentry. The rebels retired on North Walsham and Gimmingham, and, upon the approach of the bishop's forces, they farther retreated to Thorpe Market, and then, swinging round, entered North Walsham by the Antingham road, having thus, to a certain extent, turned the bishop's flank. So far I have given an epitome of Mr. Rye's account, and I cannot do better than add the rest in his own words entirely. He says, "Here they entrenched themselves, and on the earth thrown out of their trench, they piled up windows, shutters, doors, tables, and such like things, to make a barricade; while, as though to make their men fight more desperately, they blocked up their rear with their camp carts. Of how their camp was stormed we know but little; all we have are a few graphic sentences, in which the bishop is described as, lance in hand, dashing on horseback over the trench, 'grinding his teeth,' and leading the forlorn hope over the barricade, seizing Litester, sternly condemning him to death, then piously giving him absolution, and kindly holding up his head as he was dragged to an immediate gibbet; but in spite of all kindness, seeing him hanged, very tenderly but very efficaciously. A good, bold soldier this Spencer, but hardly our present idea of a bishop or an honest man—possibly not as honest a man or as good a citizen as the hanged rebel—for afterwards we find him impeached and found guilty in Parliament of accepting bribes from the French, and distinguishing himself by zealous persecutions of the Lollards.

"The scene of the massacre, and possibly of Litester's execution, was on the Norwich side of North Walsham, whither, no doubt, most of the rebels were driven out by the bishop's rush from the Antingham side of the town. The shaft of a stone cross still stands in the crook of the road to mark the spot. 'They dew say a mazin lot of men are buried in that pightle,' as a rustic once told me."

The Bishop died 23rd August, 1406; and was buried in Norwich Cathedral.

Another account says :—Henry Spencer was appointed Bishop of Norwich 1370, and was distinguished for his warlike propensities, and acquired the title of the "fighting Bishop." With great promptitude and resolution he put down the insurgents in East Anglia (1381), as general leading his men to the attack, sitting in judgment on prisoners, and ministering to them as priest before execution. Armed with full Papal authority by Urban VI. for a crusade against his rival Clement VII., Spencer engaged to serve a year against France, the supporter of Clement, and passed into Flanders early in 1388 with 5000 men-at-arms and archers. He took Gravelines and massacred the inhabitants, defeated an army of 1200 men, entered Dunkirk, and became master of the coast as far as Sluys. Failing, however, the expected reinforcements, he retired from the siege of Ypres, and returned to England. He was charged in Parliament with taking a bribe from the French (which he disproved), and with returning before his time of service was ended, and was deprived of his temporalities till he paid damages to the king. At a later period he showed his animosity to the Lollards, and swore that if any of Wickliff's preachers came into his diocese he would burn or behead them.—Cates' *Dictionary of General Biography.*

(92) "Itm̄ to M⁹ Coke for Councell." It is difficult to say who this Mr. Coke may have been, but it is quite possible that he was

Robert Coke, or Cooke, who resided at Mileham, and married
Wynifred, daughter and co-heir to William Knightley, on the 22nd
December, 1543.   They were married in the Church of S. Peter
Permountergate, Norwich, where the entry still remains.   Mr.
Knightley had a house not far from the church.   Mr. Robert Cooke
(as the name is entered in the Register) had a house in the adjoining
parish of S. Julian.   He was father to Sir Edward Coke, Queen
Elizabeth's famous Lord Chief Justice.

(93)   "Takyng downe of the rode lofte."   The Rood-loft was a loft
or gallery, at the chancel entrance, upon which the rood or cross and
its appendages were set up.   From it, briefs, citations, excommuni-
cations, and other notices were read out.   By order of Elizabeth, all
rood screens and lofts were to be removed, and this was carried out
in Elmham Church and many others, by sawing the screens asunder,
taking away the top and leaving the base, in order that there might
be something left to divide the chancel from the nave.

(94)   "Itm̃ for the X Cõmandyments."   A commission was issued
to the Ecclesiastical Commissioners in 1561, directing them, amongst
other things, "to consider the decays of churches, and unseemly
keeping of chancels, and to order the Commandments to be set up
at the east end of the chancel, to be not only read for edification,
but also to give some comely ornament and demonstration that the
same is a place of religion and prayer."—Cardwell, *Doc. Ann. LV.*
This order respecting the Commandments was repeated in the
advertisements of 1564, when they are directed to be "set up on the
east wall over the said table," *i.e.*, the Communion table.

(95)   "The bysshopps iniounccions."   No doubt the Bishop's
Injunctions related to the Commission of 1561.

[A° Dm.
1562.]

(96)   "The suite fyne of the town lands."   A payment to the
Court Manor.

(97)   " A newe saulter."   The version used in the Psalter is the

old translation of the Bible—that of Tyndale and Coverdale (1535) and Rogers (1537)—which was revised by Cranmer (1539), and published in a large volume, and placed in the churches with the royal sanction. The other portions of Scripture in the Prayer-book were taken from the last translation, at the revision in 1661. But the old Psalter was not altered: the choirs were accustomed to it, and its language was considered to be more smooth and fit for song. The custom of singing the Psalms is undoubtedly primitive.—*Procter.*

A° Dm. 1563.

(98) " The newe homelye booke." The first book of Homilies, printed by Richard Grafton, was issued the 31st July, 1547, the first year of Edward VI. A new edition was ordered to be published by Elizabeth in 1562, in which the Queen "straitly chargeth all parsons, vicars, curates, and all other having spiritual cure, every Sunday and Holyday in the year, at the ministering of the Holy Communion, or if there be no Communion ministered that day, yet after the Gospel and Creed, in such order and place as is appointed in the Book of Common Prayer, to read and declare to their parishioners plainly and distinctly one of the said Homilies, &c." An edition of the second part of the Homilies was printed by Jugge and Cawood in 1563. The entry above seems to refer to this last. Farther on in 1568, is an entry " for the *first* tome of homilies & the quiens Iniunctyons."

A° Dm. 1566.

(99) " office Lond of the teñte fos?." Office land of the tenement called " Foster's." It seems that in ancient times pieces of land were appropriated to different parochial offices. These were either granted or bequeathed by certain donors, or were set apart by the assent and consent of the Township for the purpose. They were either held by the parochial officers themselves, or were let by the churchwardens ; and the rents applied to the different salaries of the officials concerned. Thus we find a piece of land in Stuston called "Constable Acre," and in Framlingham, "Constable Pasture;" also " Dog Whipper's Land " in Barton Turf. The Dog Whipper

L

was an important church officer in former days. Whether more curs abounded then than now I know not; perhaps so, as dog licenses were then in the far distance; at all events the breed has not decreased. The Dog Whippers' duties consisted of (according to many entries in Elmham Churchwardens' books) "wiping yᵉ Dogges out of yᵉ Churche" during the hours of Divine Service, and for this he received 4s. per annum, paid quarterly.

Mr. Gomme in *Village Community* seems to be of opinion that before the historical period, when the first Aryans or Teutons came, they found a race whom they subjected to menial offices, and to them belonged of right the pieces of land called after their offices. He says: "At Aston, and in a minor degree at Malmesbury, we have already noticed that some of the villagers were set apart as village servants, paid for out of village lands, and regarded as a necessary part of the village system. Everywhere in India these servants belong to a low caste, non-Aryan race, and everywhere they help to make the Indian village communities self-supporting and independent of each other." Again: "Field allotments for village servants form a valuable portion of our early municipal history. The aldermen of Nottingham were paid by an allotment of the seventh part of a meadow to each, called the alderman's part." Among a number of instances he mentions that at Ashbury the "berebrat"* held a yardland; at Darent near Rochester the beadle held five acres as beadle, shepherd, and hayward; and the smith at Chalgrave had an acre of meadow, called Sundacre.

(**100**)    "Mᵍ straunge." This must have been Hamon le Straunge, of Hunstanton, who, at this time (1566), was lord of the manor of Gressenhall.

(**101**)    "sᵖ John franckelin, clerke." Mr. Carthew, in *Hundred of Launditch*, says:—"By deed dated 4th May, 34 Eliz., John Franklyn,

---

* The Saxon designation of the garnier or keeper of the granary.

late of Wangford, Suff., Clk., son and heir of Richard Franklyn, late of North Elmham, dec., in confirmation of a feoffment made by his father to Will. Franklyn, now of Rollsby, Gent., brother of $s^d$ John, released all right in lands in Elmham, late of $s^d$ Richard."

A° Dm. 1567. (102) "$M^9$ goggeneye." The Goggeneyes came of an ancient family. The will of Robert Goggeneye, of Brisley, bears date 8th Oct., 1505. John Goggeneye, A° 37 Hen. VIII., settled lands in Beetley on himself and Alice his wife, and the heirs of their bodies. A° 4 and 5 Phil. and Mary, after the death of Edmund, his father, he succeeded to lands in Brisley, which he devised to Alice his wife, for life, with remainder to Symon his son, in fee, and was dead before the 26th July, 1557. This Symon is no doubt the "$M^9$ Goggeneye" mentioned above. The Elmham Register contains the burial of his son Symon in 1578, and of his daughter Frances in 1579.

(103) "$M^9$ cleres balye." The Cleres or Clares also sprang from an ancient family. In the 18th year of Edw. IV., certain messuages, lands, and foldcourses in North Elmham were enfeoffed to Richard Southwell, Esq., Robert Clare, Esq., and others; and on the 8th Feb., 24 Eliz., a writ was directed to Sir Edw. Clere, Knt., " ad inquirend post mortem Hamonde Lestrange nup de Hunstanton, Ar., defunct," concerning the tenure of certain lands, some of them lying in Elmham.

A° Dm. 1568. (104) "$M^9$ taverns close." The owner of this close was no doubt James Taverner. See note 90, p. 123.

A° Dm. 1560 to 1568. (105) "A calender to the service booke." On January 22nd, 1561, Queen Elizabeth issued a Commission to Matthew Parker, Archbishop of Canterbury, and others, directing them "to peruse the order of the said Lessons throughout the whole year, and to cause some new calendars to be imprinted, whereby such chapters or parcels of less edification may be removed, and other more profitable may supply their rooms." In this Calendar the names of most of the saints were inserted which find a place in our present Prayer-book.

A° Dm.
1568 to
1571.

**(106)** "Accordinge to the statwte." Toulmin Smith's *Parish*, p. 231-233, quotes from the statute 24 Hen. VIII., cap. 10. He says, "There used to be a Committee in every Parish for the destruction of noyfull fowles and vermyn." By the above statute a rate was to be laid to raise a sum of money to be distributed to the destroyers of vermin. "For the heads of 3 old rooks, or 6 young rooks, 1*d.*; for the heads of every fox or gray (a badger), 12*d.*; for the heads of every polecat or wildcat, 1*d.*"

**(107)** "The towne net." I conclude this was a net for catching rooks. A few entries on, the parish is fined for "the towne neate." This means, no doubt, the town "cattle," which had probably done damage by straying. "Neate" = cattle, used sometimes to be spelled "net," as, for instance, the "Netmarket," or cattle market, in Norwich. It is doubtful if "net" (in its proper sense) was ever spelled "neate."

**(108)** "The Sawnce bell." The Sance, Sanctus, or Sacring Bell. The little bell rung at the Elevation of the Host, or when It is approaching in procession through the streets. Now called Sanctus Bell, from the words "Sanctus, Sanctus, Sanctus Deus Sabaoth." The word is derived from the French *sacrer*, and the old English verb *sacre*, to consecrate. "He heard a little sacring bell ring to the elevation of a to-morrow mass."—Reginald Scott's *Discovery of Witchcraft*, 1584. "The sacring of the kings of France."—*Temple.* See Brewer's *Phrase and Fable.*

A° Dm.
1549.

**(109)** "S° John Pecke." He was Vicar of Elmham from 1541 to 1559.

**(110)** "John Eluyche." See note 6, p. 93.

**(111)** "Y° plowlett." The plow light. I imagine this was the light burnt before the plow altar in the church, where husbandmen were wont to resort for the purpose of paying their devotions and making their votive offerings.

# GLOSSARY.

Accōpte : account

Acr⁹ : acre

Afᵗ : after

Agēyst : against

Alle : ale

Allowans : allowance

Alowyd : allowed

Amͨcimēt : amercement, fine

A more suñe : an additional sum

Apere : appear

Apͬll : April

Apptaynyng : appertaining

Arowes : arrows

Arrerages : arrearages, arrears (of rent)

Aulᵗ : altar

Awncyent : ancient

Badrycke, Bawdrick or Baldrick. From *baudrier*, a strap or girdle of leather fastened to a bell clapper

Bake : back

Balye : bailiff, steward

Bañer : banner

Beare : beer

Bekyn : beacon

Bell-foñder : bell-founder

Bell-soller : bell-chamber

Beneth : beneath

Ber, bere : beer

Beryng : bearing

Besyds : besides

Beying : being

Boud, bourde : board, food

Boords : boards, timber

Borners : burners

Botes : boots

Bowt : bought

Breke, bryke : brick

Brokē : broken

Bruars : brewers

Busshye : bushy

Buttalls : abuttals, boundaries

Butteres : buttresses

Bwll : bull

Bye: by ; also buy

Byeng: being

B₃ : bushel

C = 100, *i.e.* "C tyles," 100 tiles

Cādlemas: Candlemas

Campȳge-closse, cāpyng-closse : camping-close

Carienge, caryyne : carrying

Caryeg: carriage

Casse : case

Causye : causeway, path

Censors: censers, incense-vessels

Certen, certeyne, c°ten : certain

Chantryes : chantries. See note 66, p. 115

Chapitell, chapettle: capitular, *i.e.*, Capitular Court, the Court of the Dean and Chapter

Cha⁹sell: chancel

Chyrchereues: churchreve, church officer or warden

Clen: clean

Clery storys: clerestories, an upper story of windows rising *clear* above the adjoining parts of the church.

Clooke: clock

Cōcernyng: concerning

Coke : cook

Coler, collectour, colour: collector (of rents)

Comãded: commanded

Comb₃ : coombs. A coomb is a dry measure of four bushels, or half a quarter

Comō : common

Comōly : commonly

Comons, coñnos : commons, provisions

Compenye, cōpenye : company

Com̃unyō: communion

Com̃yssary: commissary

Contentacon: contentation, satisfaction

Coopes: copes or capes

Corpis x⁹ gyld: Corpus Christi Guild

Cōstables: constables

Costes : costs

Coū : council

Cōuenyet: convenient

Coũyng: covering

Cōveyyng : conveying

Creistemas : Christmas

Crocks : earthern vessels

Daggard : dagger

Deate, decte : date

Deliuid, delūid, delyūed, delyūyd:
delivered

Deptyd: departed

Donne : done

Dore : door

Drȳkyng : drinking

Dyscrecōn, dystrecōn : discretion

Diuc⁹sse, dyu⁹se : diverse

Eale : aisle

Eche : each

Elys: aisles

Entens : intents

Entre : enter

Este : east

Ester : Easter

Euynsong : evensong

Eu⁹y : every

Euyn: even, evening

Expēs: expenses

Exp⁹ssed : expressed

Eyche : each

Eyght : eight

Faldgaate, falde gate, falgate : a
gate across a public road to
prevent cattle from straying on
to other owners' property

Fayn : fain, intended

Fearme, fearmeȝ, ferme : rent.
See note 2, p. 91

Fecheynge : fetching

Feld, felde, ffuyld, ffyld : field, a
tract of arable land belonging,
under the feudal system, to the
township, and which was formerly divided in strips amongst
the householders

Felow, felowe, ffelow: fellow

Fermour, ffermer : farmer

Fersyng : ferzing, to go a furz-
ing or cutting furze on a common, or heath, is an East
Anglian expression

Fete: feet

Feyer stede : fair-sted, or a place
where a fair is held

Feyyng, fyeing : fying, East
Anglian for cleaning out. "To
fay out" a ditch appears to be
a very old word in common
use in Cheshire, Yorkshire, &c.,
as well as East Anglia. Some
say it is derived from forgire
= purgare; others that it is
Danish, i.e., feic, to sweep out

Fote : foot

Fowlde, ffould : fold, a fold-course
was a piece of land where the
lord of the manor exercised his
right to compel his tenants to
fold their sheep for the purposc

of manuring the soil; or where the tenants had a right to do the same

ffayer: fair

ffe: fee

ffest: feast

ffyer: fire

ffyrckyngs: firkins

ffysshe: fish

ffurres: furze, whin, gorse

Follynge: following

Folueth: followeth

For gotyn: forgotten

Fouñte, funte: font

Fourme: form

Fre: free

Frō, fro': from

Furder: further

Fynysshyng: finishing

Fysten: a tax, derived from "frist," to swagger or to try it on

Gaat: gate

Gaf, gafe, gaue, goofe, gyffe: gave

Gage: gauge, measure

Gardē: garden

Geer, gere: gear, the church linen, surplice, &c.

Generall: general, the Archdeacon's Court

Geven, gyfne: given

Goying: going

Gracs: grace's, i.e., His Grace's commands

Grāted: granted

Gratte, grats, g̃ts: grate, grates, a frame of parallel or cross bars

Grauell: gravel

Grauȳg, grauyng, g̃vyng: graving, i.e., cutting out

Gresse: grease

Grope: grip, a small ditch or furrow. Anglo-Saxon, grêpe, gröpe

Gudgions: gudgeons. A gudgeon is the piece of iron in the end of a wooden shaft; it is that on which a bell hangs

Hafe: have

Hāger: hanger, i.e., bell-hanger

Hangles, hengells, hēgell: hinge, hinges

Hayer: hanger, a short, broad sword incurvated at the point.

Heare: here

Heith, hethe: heath, common

Henge: hang

Hepe: heap

Her: here

Heraf?: hereafter
Hernes : harness
Hey Crosse : High Cross
Heyred : hired
Holdē : holden, held
Hole : whole
Hoped : hooped
Horsemete : horsemeat, provender
Hs : his
Hu⁹dered, hu⁹dred : hundred
Hȳ : him
Hye : high
Hyr : her


Iniounccions, iniunctyons : in-
    junctions
Inuentarye, inuētarye : inventory
Ioynctlye : jointly
I?: item


Kye : kine, cows
Kypyng : keeping


La.: labourer
Lacs : locks
Latasyng : latticing, *i.e.*, forming
    into open work like a lattice
Laten : latten, a fine kind of brass
    or bronze
Laten : letting, as applied to a
    house or land

Lawnds : clothes, church linen,
    hence laundry
Leadd, led, ledd, leed : lead (metal)
Leyt : leet
Leaton : let
Lectorn : lectern
Lestewayes : leastways
Lether : leather
Leuyed : levied
Ley : lay
Leying, leyyng, lyeing, lyyng :
    lying.
Lō ff. : londe fferme, rent of land
Lode, lods, loode : load, loads
Lond, londe : land
Longyne, longyng : belonging
Lynyng : linen


M⁹ : mister
Mad : made
Malmesaye : malmsey, wine used
    for the Holy Eucharist
Maňˀ : manner, also manor
Mandy Thrysdaye : Maundy
    Thursday, from mandatum
    (Latin), a command
Masbokes : mass-books
Masyng : mason
Mattocke : mattock, a kind of
    pickaxe, having the iron ends
    broad instead of pointed

M⁹che, marche: march (month of)

M⁹cy: mercy

M⁹cyamēt, m̃cyment: amercement, subject to a fine

Meane: mean, unskilled

Meaš, merš, meš, measer: mercer

Mēdyng: mending

Mencyoned: mentioned

Menor: manner, manure, soil. See note 8, p. 94

Midsom̃: midsummer

M⁹ket: market

Moche: much

Monethes: months

Monstrans: monstrance, a transparent pyx or box, in which the consecrated wafer or host is held up to view before the congregation. See note 53, p. 111

Mʳᵉˢ: mistress

Mye L.: my lord

Mynystryng: ministering

Natyuyte: Nativity

Neaded: needed

Neate: neat, cattle

Nether: lower

Nourcenge: nursing

Obyte: obit.   See note 28, p. 101

Ocke, ooks: oak, oaks

Oop: up

Oʳ, ouʳ, owʳ: our

Ornamēts: ornaments

Ou⁹: over

Ought, owt, owte: out

Ou⁹seer: overseer

Oynnyngs, oyñyngs: onions

Paier, payer: pair

Pāne: pan

Paue: pave

Paued: paved

Paymēt: payment

Pcell: parcell

Pchemēt, pchemyn: parchment

Pcke: park

Pctor: proctor

P⁹cynct: precinct

Pece: piece

Peyed: paid

Pformed: performed

Pfyghts: profits

Placs: places

Plat: plate

Play⁹ly: plainly

Plom⁹: plumber

Plowllett: plow light

Pmyse: promise

P⁹yssȝ: premises

P⁹r: prior

Pore : poor

P⁹oures : prior's

Ppetuytyes : perpetuities

Ppre : proper

P⁹sens : presents

P⁹sent : present

Psons : persons; also parsons

Pt, pte : part

Ptes : parts

Ptaynyng : pertaining

Ptener : partner

Pticlerlye : particularly

P⁹yce : price

Pyllors : pillars

Pysshe : parish

Pyssheners : parishioners

Pyst, p⁹yst : priest

Pytell : pightel or pightle, an enclosed piece of land, a little enclosure

Pytt : pit

Qr̄ts : quarts

Quer, quier, quyere : quire, choir

Quēste menes, queste mēs : questmen, churchwardens' assistants. See note 88, p. 122

Quethode, quethod : quetheword, bequest, legacy

Quiens : Queen's

Rearags : arrears (of rent)

Rec̃ : receipts; also received

Regist⁹ : register

Rekenyng : reckoning, delivery of accounts

Relyques, relyquys : relics

Remembruñs : remembrance

Repacon : reparation

Repaying : repairing

Reste : rest, remainder

Rivynge : riving, cutting

Rochetts. See note 7, p. 93

Rod : rode (on horseback)

Rode : rod or rood

Sacramēt : sacrament

Sawlters : psalters

Sawnce : sance or sanctus. See note 108, p. 132

Scaberd : scabbard

Sckyn : skin

Se : see

Seaynt, sent : saint

Serten, s⁹tayn, s⁹ten : certain

Seu⁹all : several

Seye : say

Sex : six

Sheos : shoes

Shest, sheste : chest

Shype : ship

Shyrplys, syrples : surplice

Skyrmysshe : skirmish
Soṁe, suṁe : sum
Soñes : sums
Sond, sonde : sand
Sones : son's
Sooles : stools
Sou⁹eyn : sovereign
Sougthe, sowthe : south
Sowd : soder or solder
Sowding : soldering
Sowl : soul
Soydyor, soydyour : soldier
Spete : spit
Spets : spits
S⁹rplusage : surplus
Statwte : statute
Staues : staves
Steyers : stairs
Steyned : stained, painted
Sthetell : kettle
Stok : stock, fund
Stolers : stoners, *i.e.*, stone gatherers
S⁹tyfycat : certificate
S⁹uant : servant
S⁹uyng : serving
Suffycyēt : sufficient
Surueyo⁹ : surveyor
Sūtyme : sometime
S⁹uyce : service
S⁹uyor : server
Swerd : sword

Sygne : sign
Syguler : singular
Syknes : sickness
Sylu⁹ : silver

Tacle : tackle
Taske : tax
Tēdyng : tending, attending to
Teen : ten
Tempre : temper
Teñ Paynott : Paynott's tenement
Teñte fost⁹ : Foster's tenement
Tery : tarry
Testamēt : testament
Thacompte : the account
Thalder : chaldron
Than : then
Tharca⁹gell, tharcangell : the Archangel
Tharrerages : the arrears
The⁹ : them, also then
Thense, thēse : thence
Ther : their, also there
Thre : three
Thuse : the use
T⁹me : term
To be stowe : to bestow
Toke : took
Toẇe : town
Trāgressours : transgressors
Tre toppe : tree top

Tybyr, tymbre: timber

Vnce: Ounce
Vntyll: until
Voyle: viol
Vytalls: victuals

Wags: wages
Wasshȳg: washing
Wer: were
Whā, whē: when
Wheale: wheel
Wher: where
Wherwᵗ: wherewith
Wheryn: wherein
Whyghtson: Whitsun
Whygt: white
Whytlether: white leather
Wodd, woodd, woode: wood
Worckemāshype, worckmāshyp: workmanship
Wᵗ: with

Wᵗin: within
Wᵗnes: witness
Wȳdows: windows
Wyer: wire
Wyghtson: Whitsun
Wyll: will
Wyues: wives

Yche: each
Yᵉ: the, y = old Saxon *th*, þ
Yearrd, yerd: yard
Yer, yere: year
Yᵉᵐ: them
Yᵉⁿ: then
Yᵉʳ, ẏ⁹: their, also there
Yerne, Yron: Iron
Yⁱˢ, yˢ: this
Yncomyng: incoming, income
Ynstrumēts: instruments
Ys: is
Yt: it
Yᵗ: that

## PROPER NAMES.

Alsehm̃: Aylsham
Alyn: Allen
Alys, Alyᵉ: Alice
And⁹son: Anderson
Añe: Anne
Annuncyacōn: The Annunciation
Annys: Agnes

Bacche: Bache or Batche
Baptyste: S. John the Baptist
Bertylmew: Bartholomew
Bew⁹leye: Beverley
Blackbrō: Blackborough
Blackhurn Fyrlong. The ter-
mination hern, hurn, or hyrne
signifies a sharply angular
field, i.e. a horn of land: Saxon,
hyrne, a nook or corner. A
furlong is a rectangular piece
of land 220 yards in breadth.
The early manors were so
divided in order to their better
management. These furlongs
were again divided into narrow
strips, containing about half-
an acre each, and separated by

baulks, or furrows. Some of
them were held by the tenants,
and some by the lord of the
manor.
Broūe: Browne
Byllyngforde: Billingford

Carbroke: Carbrook
Cateryng: Catherine
Cavston: Causton
Clemēt: Clement
Couerlecreste: Coverlecrest
Cursñ: Curson

Edgegraue: Edgegrave
Edmñd: Edmund
Elu⁹yche: Elverich
Elyn: Ellen
Erasmᶜ: Erasmus
Estagate: Eastgate
Estderhm̃: East Dereham
Eu⁹ode: Everard

ffakenhm̃: Fakenham
ffolsehm̃: Foulsham
ffrāck: Frank
ffrāckelyng: Frankelyng

Gatele : Gately

Gressenhale, Gressnall : Gressenhall

Herry : Harry, Henry

Hewghe : Hugh

How : Hoe

Jaffry : Jeffery

Jamys : James

Jooăne : Joan

Lady Hastens : Lady Hastings

Landytcher : Launditch

Lenne : Lynne

Loue : Love

Lychehm̃, Lytchm̃ : Litcham

M⁹chall : Michell

M⁹garete : Margaret

Miches, Mihelmes, Mychaelmas :
Michaelmas

M⁹tyn : Martin

Mussolde, Mushold : Mousehold

Nich, Nichūs : Nicholas

Normādy : Normandy

Norwᶜʰ : Norwich

Payford, Peinforde : Paynford

Parckgate : Parkgate

Ƥckehyrne : Parkhirne

Perymā : Peryman

Robynsñ : Robinson

Rustñ : Ruston

Ry. H. : Richard Heyward

Sand⁹ : Sanders

Shetyll : Shettell

Sohm̃, Soñe : Soham

Stephēsñ : Stephenson

Strawnges : (Le) Strange's

Swaffhm̃ : Swaffham

Swăton : Swanton

Syluerdeane : Silverdeane

Syluest⁹ : Sylvester

Taūner : Taverner

Tavern⁹s : Taverner's

Thom̃s, Thow̃se : Thomas

Thompsñ, Thōpsñ, Thōpson :
Thompson

Trēdell : Trendell

Walsynghm̃ : Walsingham

Windhm̃ : Wymondham

Wodcoke : Woodcock

Wy, Wyllm̃, Wylyam : William

Wyllsñ : Wilson

Wyssyngsett : Whissonsett

Yarā, Yarrhm̃ : Yarham

## LATIN EXPRESSIONS.

"Anno Regni Elizabeth, Angliæ Reginæ, Tertio," in the third year of the reign of Elizabeth, Queen of England

"A° Dm̃," Anno Domini, in the year of our Lord

"A° 1° Ed. Sixti," in the first year of Edward VI.

"D, di, dimidium," half

"Dñe," dominæ, Lady

"Eiusden," ejusdem, of the same

"Et sic quietᵉ est dictᵉ Tho. Powle hoc Anno," and so the said Thomas Powle is quit, i.e., for this year free from any further obligation in respect of his account

"Hoc sig̃," hoc signo, by this sign or mark

"In pᵍm̃, in pᵍmis," in primis, first

"Iℓ," item, also

"Nūc," nunc, now

Oḃ, obolus = ½d, a Greek coin.

Six οʹβολοί = one δραχμή

"Oñatʳ in libr̃ novo," Oneratur in libro novo, is filled in or entered in a new book

"Ᵽ Aⁿ," per annum

"Pᵍcedens," precedens, foregoing

"Ᵽ cõsili," per consilium, by the inhabitants in meeting assembled

"Ᵽua," parva, little

"Ᵽvt," prout, as

"Redditᵖ soluℓ," reditus solutus est, the rent has been paid

"S," scilicet, namely

"Tᵖre Natieᵖ," Terræ Nativæ, copyhold as opposed to freehold lands

"Ut hic patr," ut hic patetur, as is here made manifest

"Ut sup̃," ut supra, as above

"ꝗc," et cetera

AGAS H. GOOSE, PRINTER, RAMPANT HORSE STREET, NORWICH.